Alexander Boddy, A. F. Jacassey

To Kairwân the Holy

Scenes in Muhammedan Africa

Alexander Boddy, A. F. Jacassey

To Kairwân the Holy
Scenes in Muhammedan Africa

ISBN/EAN: 9783744755603

Printed in Europe, USA, Canada, Australia, Japan

Cover: Foto ©Lupo / pixelio.de

More available books at **www.hansebooks.com**

SCENES IN MUHAMMEDAN AFRICA.

BY

ALEXANDER A. BODDY.

ILLUSTRATED BY A. F. JACASSEY.

LONDON:
KEGAN PAUL, TRENCH & CO., 1, PATERNOSTER SQUARE.
1885.

TO MY MOTHER.

PREFACE.

O Gentle and Respected Reader,

It is reported of the Prophet Muhammed, that on a certain night he leapt upon the winged steed Al Borac, which stood neighing by the awful Bayt Allah of Mecca, and that thereupon they flew together over Arabia and Sinai until they arrived at El Kûds, the earlier Kibleh of Islam. Here Muhammed enstabled Al Borac in the Holy Rock, and mounting the Ladder of Light, he passed through the Seven Heavens, until he attained to the Lote Tree, beyond which there is no passing. Very noteworthy Suras in his "Most Perspicuous Explication" were composed after the Lailat-al-Miraj.

In later times an Imaum of another Faith mounts a chariot, drawn by a span of four fiery steeds, and beneath a burning sun he hasteth across the Sahel, towards the Mughreb, and standeth within the sacred Mihráb of Okhbah's Sanctuary. He does not ascend to the Seventh Heaven, he only gains the summit of the great Minar of Kairwân; but journeying Northwards to the Land of his Fathers, he humbly imitates Al Borac's rider, and ofttimes adding to his own the thoughts of those who are more wise, he doth pen Suras wherein the curious may read of sights and sounds which appertain to the Dar-ul-Islam.

He greeteth thee, O Gentle and Respected Reader, and craveth thy gracious indulgence, saluting thee as he hath been learned in those lands (his Hand first touching Lips and Forehead and Breast), with the peaceable benison

"SALAAM ALICÛM."

Month of El Dulkaada,
  In the Year of the Flight 1301.

CONTENTS.

CHAPTER I.
THE MECCA OF THE WEST.

PAGE

Kairwân at the British Association—The B.A. at Southport—A glimpse at the Sacred City—Its influence in Europe—Its founder—Okhbah and the snakes—Mecca's fall to be Kairwân's rise—Successful and unsuccessful visitors—Sir G. Temple—Marquess of Waterford—Dr. Tristram—Edward Rae—Lord Bective—The French army—A Christian Imaum   1

CHAPTER II.
BY OCEAN AND SEA.

A commotion on the ocean—Complimentary boatswain—Captain Brown—Martin Luther, the steward—Across the bay—The Spanish peninsula—Corunna—Cape St. Vincent—Africa—Tangiers—Old Gib.—The Sierra Nevada—Turtle-mocking—Cape Agate—Trinity Sunday—Ras Sebbah Rous—Galita and Galitona—Cape Bon—Pantellaria—Moonlight musings   10

CHAPTER III.
EL FIOR' DEL MONDO.

Elementary geography—Gozo and the Gozitans—Arabic and Maltese—Island of Malta—*Cala di San Paolo*—The place where two seas meet—St. Paul's shipwreck—The grand harbour of Valetta—H.M.S. *Inflexible*—Good-bye to the *Glenochil*—Dunsford's Hotel—Mr. Clophan—Floriana—Marketing—Off to Barbary—On board the *Ville de Rome*—Filfla as a target—Our doctor in danger—The vice-consul of Tripoli   19

CHAPTER IV.

TARABOLOS GHARB.

Approaching an African sea-port—Why called Tripoli—Pass the Turkish *Douane*—An English face—Quadrifrontal arch—Camel campanology—Yellow Moors and Blackamoors—Scenes in bazaar—Lieutenant Nedjih Beki—An awful dream—More awful awakening—*A marriage* 28

CHAPTER V.

THE CHIEF MOSQUE OF TRIPOLI.

Muhammedan prejudices—Not easily overcome—Mosque of Gordji—Interior—The *Mihráb*—The *Kibleh* of Islam—The *Membar*—Ascend the *Minar*—The *Adzán* or cry of the Mueddin—Bird's-eye view of Tripoli—Backsheesh ... 40

CHAPTER VI.

THE ESPARTO MARKET.

The Souk-el-Halfa—Camel's vocal organs—Riding a *djmil*—Rising superior—The ship of the desert—*Mal-de-mer*—Sorting esparto—Coloured ladies and gentlemen—Fifty-seven okes—El Ghrad—Cameline trot—Grateful Bedouin ... 47

CHAPTER VII.

WHITE FRIENDS AND BLACK.

The Maltese—British subjects—Our consulate at Tripoli—The French consul—Who is to have Tripoli?—Mysterious Italians—Walter Grace—Abdullah el Khartoumi—History of Miss Tinne—Her travels in Central Africa—Her tragic end—A visit to the home of Frederic—Parade of Turkish troops—Gratitude to the Sultan—Oriental band ... 53

CHAPTER VIII.

EL SCUK EL DJAMA (THE FRIDAY FAIR).

The Tuesday fair and the Friday fair—Off to Am Roos—Youthful piety—Fiery steed—Barb and *djmil* in collision—The Mesheyan oasis—Baracans and how to use them—The fair—

Haggling — *Black*smiths — Bellows — Pepper — Sneezes— *Mishmash*—Camelette—Sheep-slaughter—Native music— Hath not charms—Am Roos—Arab interior—*Legmi*—Its awful effects... 69

CHAPTER IX.

WITHIN AND WITHOUT THE WALLS OF TRIPOLI.

Infant schools—High school for Moors—Switches—Mosques— Tunisian refugees—Moslem pictures—*Rakaats*—Ablutions— Dragoot the Corsair—*Kuss-kuss-bo*—Arab Jews—Synagogues —Blood of Christian—The walls of Tripoli—View near light-house—Outside the walls—A *beer*—An odd trio—The ox and two asses—Extra-mural fair—Money changing—The orange-blossom and mothers-in-law—Harêms 82

CHAPTER X.

IN THE SAHARA.

A cavalcade—The steed of the Prophet—*Al Borâc's* trappings— His voice—Through the Mesheyah—The desert—Its colour— Bedouin and *Bindiggah*—*Hubz*—Ain Zhara—Up a *Nuklah* —*Palmam qui meruit ferat*—Trot to Tripoli—*Al Borâc's* last 96

CHAPTER XI.

VISIT TO THE PASHA OF TRIPOLI AND TO THE BLACK VILLAGE.

A dish of *sringe*—H.E. Achmet Rassim Pasha—The *nuklah* again—Story of Moslem tree-felling—Marriage and prudence —The Pasha and the murderers—Visit to negro village— Beehives—Black babies—Ethiopian salutation—Regrets and dreams 107

CHAPTER XII.

A SUNDAY IN TRIPOLI.

Sunday observance—Three sabbaths—English service—Baptisms —Florence Mary and Macdonald Nugent—The upper room—The Eleven—Christianity and Muhammedanism— Father Angelo—Madame Gagliuffi—Sunday thoughts ... 116

CHAPTER XIII.

THE LESSER SYRTIS.

The last of Tripoli—Greater and Lesser Syrtis—Acts xxvii. 17—Arab passengers on *Abd-el-Kadr*—Lotophagitis—Lotos-eaters—Why melancholy—Homt-es-Souk—Bony pyramid—Ghabes—Saharan canal—French army chaplain—Père Hyacinthe—The Salvation Army 123

CHAPTER XIV.

THE CITY OF CUCUMBERS.

Es Fakouse—"Sfax facts"—Country seats—Cucumbers—Bombardment—Mr. Leadbitter—Olive-crushing—Arab funeral—Bakery—Cisterns—Abattoirs—Bazaars—Mosques—Three old Moors—*El Hammam*—Abdul Moulir's house—*Shadushes*—Cadi—Sponges—Koran text—Ride among gardens—Mirage 133

CHAPTER XV.

MAHDIA MONASTIR, AND SUSA.

A Kairwân port—Oil on troubled waters—Cape Afrikia—A Mahdi here—Monastir and the Monastiri—Susa and black-eyed Susans—Sensible straw hats—Sunset off Susa—Musical marines—The man in the hammock 144

CHAPTER XVI.

ACROSS THE SAHEL TO KAIRWÂN.

A farewell dinner—Off to Kairwân—Obstructionists—Last view of Mediterranean—Es Sahel—Francesco Bonichi—Moureddin—Berbers—Waggons—Sheep and goats—Steppes and Sahel—Kairwân and El Kûds—Tramways—First view of the Holy City—Camel dentistry—Well near Kairwân—Snails—Tamarisks—Cicalas—Gloomy Kairwân—Camel dissection—Locanda—View from lattice—Kairwani concert 151

CHAPTER XVII.

THE HOLIEST SPOT IN AFRICA.

A cry in the night—Mueddin-roar—Inconsiderate Arabs—Enter the Holy City—The Great Mosque—Quadrangle—Roman inscription—The *Minar*—*Adzân* in English—View over Kairwân—The "Don't-know" mountains—The Holy of Holies—Pillar curse and pillar test—The *Mihráb*—The *Membar*—Roman spoils—Okhbah's dream 166

CHAPTER XVIII.

THE KAIRWÂNIS AT HOME.

An *aguz*—Imprecations—Hats and saddles—Cruelty to horses—Skin bazaar—Goats' horns—Buying carpet—*Hadadi*—Thunderstorm—African solicitor and English—Barbary barbers—*Fez* and *Sheshya*—Flies at lunch—Flocks and herds—The Renegade of Kairwân—Monk and Moslem—M. Soulié in *Figaro*—The Mahdi and Kairwân 183

CHAPTER XIX.

ENCOMPASSING THE CITY.

How to spell Kairwân—The City of Victory—Thermometer, 140 Fahrenheit—Dying camel—*Booma*—Gate of Peaches or Greengages—French camp—The Mueddin with *my* flag—The Mahdi again—Abd-el-Kader el Ghelani—The *Kasla* or *Keshla*—Suburb Jibliyeh—The Zaouia Tidjania—Mosque of the Olive Tree—A *Khaukh*—Suburb Kabliyeh—A shrunken city—Sketching the Great Mosque—The sacred well and the greyhound Baruti 198

CHAPTER XX.

SAINTLY RESTING-PLACES.

Three hairs from Muhammed's beard—Tomb of the Companion—Fanaticism—The hours of prayer—*Beni Yssou*—Son of a gun—The anchors of Noah's ark—Reduction of Sebastopol by Kairwân muzzle-loaders—Sacred swords—Sunday in Kairwân—Worshippers in the Great Mosque 210

CHAPTER XXI.

IN BEDOUIN-LAND.

Farewell to Kairwân—Drive through the Sacred City—Out on the desert plains—The mirage—A well at last—Bedouins and backsheesh—Dr. Tristram's experiences in Tunisia—Supper with the Waregrans—Bedouin hospitality and insect life—El Menarah—Beer-el-Buwita 220

CHAPTER XXII.

A NIGHT IN A KHAN.

The African traveller at Bir-el-Buwita — Fellow-travellers — Bedouin camp fire—Insect horrors—A British subject—*En route* to Tunis—Barley harvest—El Khwin—Kroumbalia—Hammam el Enf—Thascius Cyprianus—A Simoon—The fire-horse—Camel dumpling—Farewell to Bedouin-land ... 233

CHAPTER XXIII.

TUNIS, CARTHAGE, AND BIZERTA.

Morals at Tunis—Scene from hotel windows—The bazaars—Story-tellers—Jew children at school—Serpent-charmers—Author of "Home, sweet home"—To Carthage by rail—The lost slippers—On the Byrsa—Gulf of Carthage—Æneas—The Tyrians—Hasdrubal—Perpetua and Felicitas—St. Cyprian—St. Augustine—Bizerta—Jacassey 243

CHAPTER XXIV.

THE HOME OF AUGUSTINE.

Algeria—Al Kalah—Bonah—Ubba—Broken cisterns—Statue of St. Augustine—His "Confessions"—Thagaste—Monica—Carthage—Milan—The great Bishop of Hippo Regius—His life and death—A swim—Fishing boats—A rude picture—Our drive—Farewell to Africa—Sardinia—Straits of Bonifacio —Corsica—Ajaccio—Napoleon—Beaune—Snores—Rhone —Musical mastication—Across *La Manche*—Westminster Abbey 259

LIST OF ILLUSTRATIONS.

Route Map	*To face title*
(*Drawn by A. F. Jacassey.*)	PAGE
Scene in Bazaar. The Story Teller ... ... *To face*	34
An Arab Interior ... ... ,,	79
On the Sahel. Sidi el Hani in the Distance ,,	160
Muhammed ... ... ,,	173
Straw Hat of the Djerîd ... ... ,,	184
Bedouin ,,	230
Oriental Concert ... ... ,,	246
Fellow-Passengers on the "Ville d'Oran" ,,	267

(*The scene stamped upon the cover is from a sketch of the Bab-el-Djülladin made by the Author at Kairwân.*)

TO KAIRWÂN THE HOLY.

CHAPTER I.

THE MECCA OF THE WEST.

Kairwân at the British Association—The B.A. at Southport—A glimpse at the Sacred City—Its influence in Europe—Its founder—Okhbah and the snakes—Mecca's fall to be Kairwân's rise—Successful and unsuccessful visitors—Sir G. Temple—Marquess of Waterford—Dr. Tristram—Edward Rae—Lord Bective—The French army—A Christian Imaum.

"He that journeyeth seven times unto Käyrawan the Holy is as he that kisseth the Kaaba of Mecca."*—*Kairwani tradition.*

MEMBERS of the British Association will remember a most interesting paper which was read in Section E on the history of the Sacred City of Africa, Kairwân the Holy, last year by the author of "The Country of the Moors." Some perhaps will recollect the

---

* A previous traveller, who entered Kairwân when a sealed city, finds that his servant and himself have acquired the right to regard themselves as ·143 of an Hadji each, "which circumstance," he adds, "affords us a certain satisfaction."

chairman (Dr. Tristram) afterwards calling upon the writer of these present sketches to speak of his journey to that Sacred City, from which he had more recently returned.

Since the meeting in Southport he has completed the revision of his journal, and now offers to the reader some of his experiences in the Pashalik of Tripoli and the Beylik of Tunisia.

An important portion of these sketches is devoted to Tarabolos Gharb—Tripoli in the West—for little has been written in late years of this fascinating neighbourhood; the subject of the "Sanctuary of the Moors" is, however, especially dwelt upon, as to which now a few preliminary words.

About one hundred and twenty miles due south from the ruins of Carthage stand the white crenellated walls of this once mysterious city, "the holiest spot in Muhammedan Africa," *M'dint el Kairwân el Mahrota* —Kairwân the well-guarded.

At the foot of the Ousselat Mountains, it rises from the desert-like plain all quivering with heat, and dotted with stunted tamarisks, mosques and colleges, *Djâmas*, *Záouias*, and *Medressas*, all white and blazing, o'ertopped by the huge square *Minar* of the Djâma 'l Kebir.

Of its appearance, more hereafter; but first a few words on the history of Kairwân.*

---

* A most exhaustive history of Kairwân is to be found in "The Country of the Moors," pp. 246-267.

From the foundation of this city, some forty years after the Hedjra or "Flight" (that is, the escape of Muhammed* from Mecca to Medina, from which all Moslems reckon their dates), Kairwân has ever been a sacred city, within whose gates no Unbeliever, whether Christian, Jew, or idolater, might enter.

Its *Záouias* and *Medressas* are the head-quarters of Moslem confraternities, which extend in a network all over the Muhammedan world, having an untold influence on the progress of events in the Dar-ul-Islam.

The history of Kairwân is of especial interest to Europeans, because of the links by which it is bound to Spain through the Moorish conquest. The world-renowned Mezquita of Cordova was built upon the plan of El Djâma 'l Kebir at Kairwân;† and Tarik, who went forth from this city, gave his name to one of Britain's mightiest strongholds, the Rock of Tarik—Gibr-al-Tar, or Djebel Tarik. In the house of many an old Moorish family hangs the key of a Spanish home, never more to turn in the lock to which it once belonged.

Built soon after the Prophet's death, when the first great wave of Muhammedanism swept towards the West, Kairwân has ever been held the most

---

* I adopt this spelling because it represents the pronunciation constantly heard in Tripoli and Tunisia.

† This has been dealt with in a paper by Mr. R. H. Carpenter, F.R.I.B.A., to which special reference is made hereafter.

sacred of African cities, the centre of Western Islamism. The history of its foundation by "Okhbah ben Nafi Ben Abdullah Ben Kaïs el Fahri" is given us by the Arabian historian Novairi. It is interesting, if not entirely credible. It has been translated into French, from which I quote a passage or two:—

"Okhbah ben Nafi, having resolved to found the town "of Kairwân, conducted his soldiers towards the place "that he had chosen, a thick jungle, through which no "path had ever been traced. His soldiers said to him "when he ordered them to begin work—'What! "wouldest thou make us construct a town in the "midst of an impenetrable forest? Shall we not be in "danger from the wild beasts of every kind, and the "serpents, whose attacks we should have to brave?' "Okhbah, whose intercession was all-powerful with "the Divine power, addressed himself then to the "Most High God (his warriors answering Amen to his "invocations). 'O you serpents and savage beasts, "let it be known that we are the companions of the "prophet of Allah! Depart from the place that we "have chosen to establish ourselves in. If we find "any of you henceforward on this spot ye shall be "put to death.' When he had ceased speaking the "Mussulmans saw with astonishment, during the "whole day, the venomous reptiles and ferocious beasts "retreating far away, and carrying with them their "young, a miracle which converted a great number "of Berbers to Islamism."

Leo Africanus, the old Moorish historian, tells us—
"Cairaoan conditorem habuit Hucba, qui universi
"exercitus dux ex Arabia deserta ab Hutmeno pon-
"tifice tertio missus fuerat; neque aliam ob causam
"conditum fuisse dicunt, quam ut in eo exercitus cum
"omni praeda Barbaris atque Numidis adempta, secure
"se continere possent."* (Leo, p. 223.)

Here, then, Okhbah and his soldiers could enjoy their loot, far away from the fleets of Christendom, but ready to sally forth whenever an opportune occasion arrived.

Burton tells us ("Mecca and Medina," vol. i. p. 10) that one day Mecca will fall before Kairwân. He perhaps quotes Bruce, who quotes a Moslem prophecy, that when the birthplace of the Prophet falls into the hands of the infidel, Alexandria will for a time succeed to its honours. "In its turn it will "be followed by *Kairawan, in the Regency of Tunis;* "and this eventually by Raschid or Rosetta, which "last will endure to the end of time."

Though almost unknown in Europe, the sacred city of Okhbah has exercised the greatest power in

---

* "The famous citie of Cairaoan, otherwise called Carven,
"was founded by Hucba, who was sent generall of an armie
"out of Arabia Deserta, by Hutmen (Othman), the thirde
"Mahumetan Califa; neither was it built (they say) for any other
"purpose, but onely that the Arabian armie might securely
"rest therein with all such spoiles as they woone from the Bar-
"barians and Numidians." (From an old translation of the works of Leo the Moor, quoted by Mr. Rae.)

Moslem Africa, and has been the "veritable Metropolis of the Crescent" in the West. For a thousand years no 'Cut-off One' entered its holy precincts; and even to the present day comparatively few Englishmen have entered Kairwân.

Sir Grenville Temple, arriving in 1830 with a strong escort, and carrying an order from the Bey of Tunis, was only allowed to pass hurriedly through the streets, and warned not to look about him. The Marquess of Waterford ten years later tried to enter, but was stoned and almost killed. The well-known Palestinian traveller, Dr. Tristram, after his wanderings south of the Atlas in 1857, visited the land of Tunis; and it is greatly to be regretted that an account of his explorations was not given to the world.* Whilst journeying in the interior of the country he circled round Kairwân's white walls, but deemed it prudent not to enter the city, though holding the necessary letter of commendation from the Bey. His travels were extended to the far south of Tunisia, through districts never previously traversed by a European, and in times when the Bedouins were far less amenable to authority than in the present day.

In 1877, bearing the requisite *Amar* from Muhammed es Sadek, Mr. Edward Rae paid a more successful visit, which was marked both by pluck and

* An account of his experiences with the Waregrans is, however, given at pp. 225–228.

kindly good humour. He was the guest of the Caid, Sidi Muhammed el Mourâbet, a descendant of the Almoravides, and during his stay he won the hearts of many Kairwanis by his pleasant manner. Mr. Rae was the first European who ventured to make a thorough plan of the city and the great mosque, and he exposed himself to serious danger in making the survey of the walls almost unaccompanied. He did not know what use would be made of the plan, or as a good Arabophile he would have torn up the much-treasured paper. When the French army in 1881 advanced on Kairwân the map thus made was their only guide. Mr. Rae had to return without entering the Djâma 'l Kebir or other mosques, yet he obtained so much information on every subject that his charming book, "The Country of the Moors," is invaluable as a guide to all the places he visited.

In April, 1881, Lord and Lady Bective, with an armed escort, entered the gates and passed through the streets of Kairwân. Six months later, General Etienne, commanding one of the three divisions of the French "Armée d'Occupation," which was to march upon and seize the Holy City, appeared outside its walls. From the great *Minar* a frightened Mueddin waved a piece of white calico, and Sidi Mourâbet, the governor, rode out of the Bab et Tunes to surrender the Holy City. When twenty-two thousand men were marching upon the city, what was he to do? The whole population does not exceed fourteen thousand souls, and the warlike members of the Zlass tribes had fled that morning to the south. So the French troops marched in at the Tunis gate, their bands playing the "Marseillaise," and passing through the principal streets came out again by the Bab-el-Djûlladin.

Seizing this opportunity, Mr. Alexander Broadley, an English barrister living at Tunis, subsequently the advocate of Arabi Pasha, visited the city as special correspondent of the *Times*,* in company with M. Galea our Vice-consul at Susa, and M. Jacassey the Tunisian artist.† Armed with the chassepot-key they saw sights that no Christian had ever yet beheld, and in his attractive work, "The Fourth Punic War," its author describes with graphic pen his experiences in the Holy City. At this time photographs were taken in Kairwân, and even in the great mosque itself.

The religious susceptibilities of the Kairwanis received a terrible shock when they saw the infidel soldiers in their sacred streets; but they have recovered now, and Kairwân is almost herself again.

* See *Times*, October 13th and November 18th, 1881.

† In *Harper* for May, 1884, is a paper from the pen of Mr. A. F. Jacassey (now of Minnesota, U.S.A.), which most picturesquely describes Kairwân. He says, "It is to-day, with "the exception of Mecca, the only city where one finds the "characteristic type of the Arab, the traditionary lore of the "race, and epics of its origin, intact as in the primitive days of "Islamism." From which it will be seen that Kairwân is worthy of some attention.

Much as they hate the intrusion of the "Roumi," yet they will hesitate ere they stone him as they stoned the Marquess of Waterford, lest reprisals follow.

The infidel having once been permitted to enter the Djâma 'l Kebir, its great doors may be swung back again if the Ferik so command; but the *Câfer* must run the risk of being smitten by any fanatic who may see him pass thence, or of being marked by some jealous member of the Aïssaouia.

The words of Victor Guerin, written in 1861, are practically true now, with the exception of the italicised portion.

"Là, jamais le Muedzin, en annonçant la prière "du haut des minarets, n'a rencontré de son regard "indigné aucun autre symbole religieux arboré sur un "sanctuaire rival, où le nom de Mahomet ne fût point "invoqué; là, depuis douze siècles, l'iman, interprète "et apôtre du Coran, *n'a jamais vu paraître en sa* "*présence un ministre de l'Evangile.*"

CHAPTER II.

BY OCEAN AND SEA.

A commotion on the ocean — Complimentary boatswain— Captain Brown—Martin Luther, the steward—Across the bay—The Spanish peninsula—Corunna—Cape St. Vincent—Africa—Tangiers—Old Gib.—The Sierra Nevada—Turtle-mocking—Cape Agate—Trinity Sunday—Ras Sebbah Rous—Galita and Galitona—Cape Bon—Pantellaria—Moonlight musings.

GLORIOUS green-blue rollers with ceaseless charge came rushing on to meet us as the *Glenochil* bravely climbed their glassy sides to plunge again from the summit into the eddying valley beyond. Down went her bows as if to the bottom of the ocean, her stern high up in air, the screw whizzing round; then came a curling, threatening wave-monster, balancing its crest aloft for a moment erect, to fling its tons of crystal dashing water on the forecastle deck.

> "The great green lines of the swift strong sea
> Came by like charges of cavalry,
> With their coats of mail and their snowy crests,
> And they bear us up on their mighty breasts;
> And the mighty breakers tower and curl,
> Marbled with emerald and pearl."*

---

* The Bishop of Bedford in *Good Words*.

Nothing could be more inspiring than to stand on the flying bridge and view one of the grandest sights in creation, as the wave mountains of the Atlantic ever rolled past, or to sit on the upper topsail yard as it swung from port to starboard, looking down on the vast tract of heaving waters, bounded only by the distant horizon circle, where the green-blue sea met the grey-blue sky dappled with fluffy cloudlets all torn and wind-driven.

A year before, the vessel I was sailing in (the *Cyprus*), was in great danger in this same Bay of Biscay, during one of the worst gales known for fifteen years, but on the *Glenochil* we experienced nothing beyond a tossing.

"Beg pardon, sir," says the boatswain; "you'll excuse the liberty, sir, but I think they spoilt a good sailor when they made you a parson." This remark was made one day upon descending from my seat on the upper topsail yard by one of the stays. He had found out that I knew the starboard-vang from the fore trysail, and a buntline from a tripping line. We soon became strong friends, and I did not find the sailors less appreciative when we had our services because I sometimes gave a hand at hauling the braces, or kept above deck in dirty weather clad in oilskins and sou'-wester.

Warm-hearted fellows are these Jack-tars, and though some were put on board hopelessly drunk, the tears would glisten quickly in their eyes, when one spoke plainly and kindly to them on solemn subjects. We had very hearty services on the *Glenochil*. Captain Brown, one of the finest specimens of the British shipmaster it has been my lot to meet, conducts service himself twice a Sunday, and lives up to his services on week days.

Of course I became chaplain in ordinary to the *Glenochil*, and all hands came to church. A strange mistake was made by Martin Luther, our Swedish steward, one Sunday. I had preached from Acts xxvii. 44—"And so it came to pass that they escaped all safe to land." I noticed that Martin was listening most attentively, though his knowledge of English was limited. Later on in the day he was reading to me out of his Swedish Bible, and stopping awhile we were talking of Swedish preachers, and comparing notes as to some of the churches at Stockholm. Then suddenly he said, "Was you really in that ship, sir, that went aground at Malta?" Well, I tried to explain as best I could that it was a long time ago that the shipwreck happened, and that it was a preacher called Paul whom I had been speaking of; but it was all to no effect. "Yes, there's a good many ships has been lost there lately, sir," he replied, as he proceeded to give me a list of the same.

He was a droll fellow, this same Martin Luther. He laughed so loudly at our feeble jokes, when he was waiting in the cabin, that one was in momentary fear of having the soup-tureen emptied down one's neck, or one's head anointed with gravy.

Over the trackless sea we plunged on our way, and for three days after the white cliffs of England had gone down below the horizon, we were out of sight of land. At last, on the third day, the dark mountains of North-Western Spain rose on our port bows, and a fine view opened out of the coast from Cape Ortegal to the Cisargas Islands.

Later on we were abreast of Corunna. Dark chocolate cliffs rise rugged and precipitous from the water's edge. An opening in the mountain range here leaves a level plain on which Corunna rests. Now and then a pretty Spanish village was seen nestling in a sandy bay, its white houses clustering round a church, the cattle descending a red road on the mountain side, as the evening called them home.

Towards noon the following day we were approaching Cape St. Vincent, the most westerly point in the continent of Europe, the scene of the great naval engagement in 1805. Bright bursts of sunshine alternated with heavy showers, while the dark blue sea was lashed into little white horses by a strong headwind. Threatening masses of cloud, piled one upon another, half obscured the sky, which looked purer and brighter as these dark vapour mountains with snowy summits reared their heads into the blue expanse.

A long dark line of grey-brown cliff extends to

the north as far as the eye can see, and to the southward runs out a wave-dashed promontory very like Flamborough Head, bearing a white lighthouse on its extreme point, and surrounded by a Portuguese building of slightly ecclesiastical style, which is a Nunnery.

Splash! splash! came some warning drops, and in a moment the sea was hissing under a tremendous downpour, and all was hidden from view. The decks swam under the waterfloods, but at last it passed away to leeward, and as the storm curtain lifted, the brown rocks of Portugal stood out all rugged, bathed in bright sunshine.

Just a week from the day when we sailed down the North Sea, we saw once more the brown-green hills of Africa before us in the early morning light, stretching from Cape Spartel to cloud-capped Abyla.

Owing to a strong 'Levanter,' we hugged the African coast in steaming through the straits. If there had been a 'Ponenter' blowing, we should have kept the mid-channel, as we should have had it with us instead of in our teeth.

Tangiers is very Oriental in character, though Occidental in position. A circling wall encloses the minarets and white flat-roofed houses, rising one above the other in endless tiers on the hill, the tower of the *Kasbah* dominating all. On the mountain sides to the west are perched pretty villas, the country residences of the consuls, etc., and to the east of the town is a fine stretch of sandy beach, a favourite promenade of the Tangerenes.

A few hours more, and we were nearing old Djebel-el-Tarik, the rock-fortress of that fierce old Kairwani, who took so large a share in the subjection of Spain to the Moors—he who went forth from Okhbah's mosque at Kairwân to carry the faith of Muhammed and the supremacy of Islam to the Lands of the North. This mountain of Tarik,—Gibraltar, the Calpe of olden times, and Abyla, the Apes mountain across the Straits, are the two Pillars of Hercules—the end of the earth and sea.

We stood in close to the town of Gibraltar, and all the familiar places opened out as we approached Europa Point. Across the bay, and beyond the neutral ground, is Algesiras, the first Spanish town, while under the shadow of the great Rock nestle Gibraltar and Rosia, all bristling with guns, which also peep out from cavern-like holes in the Rock itself—"*los dientes de la vieja*" (the old woman's teeth).

Steaming on into the Mediterranean, we saw the back of the Rock, the eastern and uninhabited side, standing out precipitous, bare, rugged, and grand in outline, like a crouching lion. Three summits there are—the most southern, Sugar-loaf Point, on which is O'Hara's Tower (1439 feet); the middle elevation, called the Signal Station (1276 feet); and the landward or northern summit, whence the sunset gun fires (1350 feet).

Over the deepest blue water we ploughed our way as we sailed under the bright hot sun over the Midland Sea, and the Sierra Nevada lifted their snow-covered heads thousands of feet into the sky as we steamed along the southern coast of Spain.

Leaning over the bows I watched the graceful porpoises shooting through the crystal water, as they fled before the swift bows of the *Glenochil*. A great turtle slowly paddled out of the way, utterly disgusted with these fussy, noisy appliances of an infidel civilization. "*Ya kelb ibn kelb?*" he seemed to say to me: "Why dost thou thus disturb my post-prandial nap?" So he moved off in a surly fashion, to bask more quietly elsewhere.

The next morning we left Cape Agate on our port quarter, and steamed all day over an oily sea, until the African hills were abeam in the evening. The dog-watches I often spent with the sailors, and taught them to play upon a set of handbells which I had brought for their amusement; the chimes and tunes rang out very sweetly over the calm sea in the evening.

I shall not forget the evening of Trinity Sunday, after our hearty services, as I leant over the bulwarks, watching the sunset hues upon the African mountains and listening to the men singing hymns on the forecastle.

We were a few miles from the promontory of the Seven Capes, in Algeria—Ras Sebbah Rous. The dark, rocky mountains were empurpled by the crimson sunset hues. The plain of rippling water stretching from us to the lighthouse at the foot of the crags changed from a dark blue where the waves leapt back from the ship's sides, to a pale green near the shore. The sky, like a flamingo's blushing breast, near the horizon passed by delicate changing hues through orange and emerald-green to grey-blue overhead. The sun, a dazzling mass of fire, rested for a moment on the molten waves, and threw a fiery track across the western sea. As soon as it set all was changed—the mountains disappeared in the mist, and the moon shone out on pale waves.

Two rocky islands lie in the track of vessels sailing from Gibraltar to Malta. They are called Galita and Galitona, and are separated only by a channel a quarter of a mile wide. Early one morning we entered these straits, and we seemed to be overshadowed by the rocky heights towering above us on either side. Most piratical looking islands they are; indeed, once they were the resort of the Tripolitan corsairs when wishing to careen their vessels or lay in fresh water.

That evening we approached the land of Tunisia, but only to leave it again, for the *Glenochil* could not put in even to oblige her only passenger. We crossed the Gulf of Carthage, and made Ras Addar, after passing under Zembra, the zebra-striped island which, with its smaller sister Zembrotta, guard the entrance to this Gulf of Tunis or Carthage.

C

Cape Bon, the Promontorium Mercurii of the Romans, and the Ras Addar of the Moors, is the northern extremity of the Dakkul promontory (from Dakkul, *strip* or *corner*), which extends to this point from Hammamet, the Town of Doves. Stern and rugged were the serrated cliffs in the evening light, as they rose 1176 feet from the sea, and crowned by a Punic cairn on the summit. A soft downy bed of snowy clouds clung to the sides of the Cape, and was tinged with a golden light from the west. Four hundred and fifty feet from the sea stands the white lighthouse whose flashing light, white and red, guides the steamers on this highway of nations, as the rude Pharos on the summit of old directed the Carthaginian galleys entering the gulf.

It was towards midnight when we were off the island of Pantellaria, and an almost dazzling full moon lit up the sea as in broad daylight. It was my last evening at sea, and I felt sad as I sat aloft, the great sails swelling out beneath me before the breeze, and casting weird shadows on the sea beneath. The outlook at the bows strode to and fro, only a little black shadow far away down below on the forecastle; the mate on the bridge with his night glass was looking at the black outline of Pantellaria, while the man at the wheel amidships directed our good vessel on her rushing course, as her red and green lamps glared out on the dark water.

CHAPTER III.

EL FIOR' DEL MONDO.

Elementary geography—Gozo and the Gozitans—Arabic and Maltese—Island of Malta—*Cala di San Paolo*—The place where two seas meet—St. Paul's shipwreck—The grand harbour of Valetta—H.M.S. *Inflexible*—Good-bye to the *Glenochil*—Dunsford's Hotel—Mr. Clophan—Floriana—Marketing—Off to Barbary—On board the *Ville de Rome*—Filfla as a target—Our doctor in danger—The vice-consul of Tripoli.

CAN we wonder that the Maltese loves to call his island home the "Flower of the World"? Barren and desolate as the yellow rocks may appear from the sea, the scene is completely changed when once one glides under the guns of St. Elmo, and finds one's self in the bright harbour of Valetta, surrounded by the innumerable *dghaisas* which flit over the blue water.

Two larger islands and two smaller ones form our Maltese dependencies. The largest, Malta, is about seventeen miles long and nine miles at its broadest part, in shape somewhat like a sole. Gozo, the sister isle, is nine miles long and five broad, and is in shape like an egg. It is only separated from

Malta by a narrow channel containing the two small islands, Comino and Cominotto. Let me attempt some description of the group of rocky excrescences upon the blue face of the Mediterranean, under whose cliffs we sailed that warm May morning.

About half-past ten, up to which time I had been busily engaged in packing up, I came on deck to find the *Glenochil* approaching Gozo's yellow cliffs.

Before us was Ras San Dimitri, the most westerly point of the islands, and high up on the hills the Guirdan lighthouse and signalling station. As the *Glenochil* was to replenish her bunkers at Valetta, Captain Brown here signalled the number of tons required, and the message was flashed to the depôts, where all was made ready for her arrival at the Grand Harbour a couple of hours later.

The capital of Gozo is Rabato, perched up on the backbone of the rocky island, which is crowded with cities, churches, and inhabitants. The latter are very industrious. The Gozitans fish for tunny, cultivate barley and cotton, and make cheeses from the milk of long-necked, long-legged sheep. They speak an Arab dialect, like their Maltese brethren. All the geographical names take one to Barbary: *ras* for cape, *oued* for ravine, stream, or river; their very salutation, *Salaam glakicum* ("peace be with you"), almost identical with the Bedouin benison. So we steamed past the hills of Gozo, crowned with ancient towns and churches, its barren-looking yellow lands divided continually into strips by the parallel stone walls built to protect the crops from the much-dreaded *mistral*.

Before us lay Gozo's big sister, Malta, stretching to the south-east, and passing the small islets, Comino and Cominotto, we were soon abreast of Ras Lahrash and Melleha Bay.

In the days when wild thyme was abundant on the hills round Melleha, it was famed for its delicately flavoured honey. Indeed it is said by many that the whole island of Melita thus obtained its ancient name—a fairly probable conjecture.

Upon the adjoining promontory is Selmûn Palace, which looks down upon the scene of St. Paul's shipwreck; and as we steamed onwards the *Glenochil* was soon passing the "certain bay with a creek," and "the place where two seas meet." An almost unanimous concensus of nautical and Biblical authorities has for many weighty reasons found, in the Cala San Paolo, the scene of the apostle's shipwreck, and in the channel between Selmûn Island (or "Gzier") and the mainland, the place where the great Alexandrian vessel was hurled ashore in the early morning light.

It is still more interesting to approach the bay from the land, where you see how exactly it satisfies all the required conditions, suggested by the Bible narrative. The splendid monograph of James Smith of Jordan hill ("Voyage and Shipwreck of St. Paul") has obtained a world-wide reputation, and a study of his arguments, together with some previous knowledge of the surroundings of the Cala di San Paolo, has made me more than ever satisfied that this is the "τόπος διθάλασσος" of Acts xxvii. 41.

Seven miles more and our voyage was practically ended, as we lay off Valetta. St. John's Cathedral, the Governor's palace, and the white forts rose from the blue Mediterranean, while the pilot, in his gaily painted *dghaisa*, came out to us over the dancing waves.

Slowly the great *Glenochil* glided under the guns of St. Elmo, her Union Jack proudly floating in the breeze, and once more we were in the Grand Harbour of Valetta,* looking upon a most picturesque scene, that strange mixture of England, Africa, and Italy.

The dark blue waves breaking over the rocks at the entrance of the harbour, rolled along in a heavy swell, lifting the rows of gondola-like *dghaisas*, all brilliant with their coloured sides and high prows. The Maltese boatmen execrated as their craft were dashed against one another and against the quay. One could never grow weary of gazing at that moving crowd; was there ever such a cosmopolitan gathering?—Arabs, Turks, Capuchins, red-coated English soldiers, Algerians, Maltese lazzaroni, black

* When St. Paul left Malta he must have sailed from Valetta, for there is no other natural harbour where the Alexandrian grain-ship could have wintered.

coats and sun helmets, priests, men-o'-war's men with un-English countenances, and policemen in semi-military costume.

Out in the harbour were modern men-of-war, with iron sides and threatening grey turrets, a contrast to those 'wooden walls' which fought for us in days gone by, and now stand high out of the water, serving as hospitals, etc., for our sailors. Rows of black screw-steamers of the unmistakable North Country type lay along the quay, taking in "bunker" coal, and hurrying off in an hour or two to Constantinople, Suez, or Newcastle. White forts and balconied houses high above us were perched on the rock, and reflected the bright sunlight, while the bells of San Giovanni and other churches were clanging in an irregular purposeless strain.

Through the hot streets I hurried to get my letters, and to make inquiries as to the steamers for Tripoli, and at last down the stair streets to the Marina, passing the flocks of goats waiting with their tinkling bells for some one to come and milk them, and so through the deep archway and past the gushing fountain out on to the quay.

In a *dghaisa* manned by two swarthy Maltese we glided over the blue waters of the Grand Harbour towards the white sides of the *Glenochil*, where they were still busy coaling, for I wished to say good-bye to my sailor friends. Passing under the sides of H.M.S. *Inflexible*, where all was excitement and hurry, as she was about to sail for Corfu, I felt almost justified in going on board and getting in every one's way. It certainly was interesting to stand in the turrets of a vessel which took such a prominent part in the bombardment of Alexandria the other month.

I was shown how to sight the 81-ton guns, and tried to imagine them pointing at Arabi's forts instead of at Mr. Eynaud's office on the Marina. The tar who took me round became most descriptive, and made me feel what an important part he had played in the subjection of Alexandria. I saw one of "Arabi's pills," a huge cylindrical shot which burst its way in, killing an officer and taking off a carpenter's legs. It is preserved as a curiosity, lying on a polished wooden rest amidships, near the aquarium. We went all over the ship; down in the holds, among the shot and torpedoes, in the engine rooms, where steam was being got up and where a very civil engineer showed me the electric machines which now and then kill off an odd man or so, up in the "conning" tower, and everywhere where one could go who takes kindly to a sailor's life. Having decorated the palm of my brave attendant with a Victorian medal, I slung myself down into the *dghaisa*, and away we dashed to the *Glenochil*. Boats were crowded round her, coal barges were leaving, and steam was up.

On the bridge of the *Glenochil* we slowly passed

down the lovely harbour, and swept out from the smooth water till we rounded Ricasoli point, and were among the tossing waves. "Good-bye! God bless you all!" and so, with many a hearty grip from rough hands, I left my good friends and clambered down the rope ladder to the pilot's boat.

Dunsford's Hotel in the Strada Reale is one of the most comfortable in Valetta. The company is ever changing, fresh faces every day at the dinner table. Bronzed Indians, rushing home by P. and O. boat just a few hours on shore; others on their way out to India or Egypt; some just come as far as Malta for the benefit of the voyage, and a few staying some time in Valetta.

I determined to make friends with the first person who sat down by me. For a long time I thought there would be an empty seat, but a rather military looking man came in and seemed to wish to be quiet. After several colloquial shots, some very wild, at last I brought him down, and we were bosom friends for the rest of our joint stay.

Mr. Clophan, of Alexandria, is well known in the Levant, and his adventures during the siege were entertaining. He had been "massacred" once or twice by the Arabs, who inconsiderately beat him over the head with bottles.

After dinner we strolled out in St. George's Square, in front of the Governor's palace, where all the fashion of Valetta was promenading. I invested in a neat six-barrelled revolver, and a thick serviceable stick, to be my companions on the Dark Continent.

In the moonlight we walked and talked, turning our steps to Floriana, one of the four or five suburbs of Valetta. We passed under the Porta Reale, its great white gateway reminding one of a Roman Triumphal Arch, and crossed the deep fosse beyond the ramparts.

An early visit to the Valetta market next morning was a treat. Crowds surrounded us during the financial arguments between my friend and the natives, and Maltese women under their *faldettes* smiled at the efforts of the *Inglizi* to reduce the price of some canaries in cages.

Up and down the picturesque flights of steps, about which Byron wrote so savagely—

> "Adieu, ye cursed streets of stairs.
> How surely he who mounts you swears!"

It is not every one, however, who has a club foot like the irritable poet.

Late that afternoon we were both steaming in different directions, my Alexandrian friend with his canaries sailing Eastwards, I, with my revolver and thick stick, on board a fine steamer of the *Compagnie Générale Transatlantique*, bound for Barbary.

I watched Malta sink into the sea, when we had sailed round its eastern extremity and seen its southern shores stretching towards Gozo. There is a little island on this side called "Filfla," from the Moorish word *filfel*, a peppercorn. I was often puzzled to know where the stormy petrels had their habitation. The mystery is solved at last. Filfla is said to be their home.

It is too bad (for the sake of that much-abused bird) that this rock of Filfla should be used as a target by men-o'-war, but this is the case. A lady in Valetta thinks "the ships would be much more usefully employed in giving dances in the Grand Harbour than in firing shots at Filfla."

At dinner I was in momentary fear for the ship's doctor, whom I was sure would enlarge his mouth from the vigorous manner in which he handled his knife. When dessert came, *M. le Medecin* seized a large apricot, and placing both elbows on the cloth he held the fruit in ape-fashion, glared at it, and then made a bite, turned it round, glared, and bit again.

A middle-aged gentleman sat on the opposite side of the saloon table. After hearing my French, he looked very hard at me, and at last he said, "Why, you're an Englishman, aren't you?" It was Mr. Taylor, the vice-consul at Tripoli, returning to Africa after a long absence.

All that evening we talked together, and far into the night, pacing the upper deck, as the *Ville de Rome* sped over the calm dark sea. Mr. Taylor in his earlier days was at Dahomey, and there was instrumental in stopping the human sacrifices.

CHAPTER IV.

TARABOLOS GHARB.

Approaching an African sea-port—Why called Tripoli—Pass the Turkish Douane—An English face—Quadrifrontal arch —Camel campanology—Yellow Moors and Blackamoors —Scenes in bazaar—Lieutenant Nedjih Beki—An awful dream—More awful awakening—A marriage.

THE chief town in the Pashalik of Tripoli lay before us next morning, stretched along the hot burning shore, as the *Ville de Rome* circled round the jagged rocks which might so easily make an excellent breakwater for the harbour of Tripoli in the West.

Glaring white were the mosques and minarets of this African city, with its background and fringe of feathery date-palm. A long line of sand stretched to the north-west, hot and red under the morning sun. On the reef of dark brown rocks surrounding the harbour the dark blue sea was breaking viciously as we felt our way to the anchorage, having taken a native pilot on board. To the east the low red cliffs are crowned with a small forest of palms, and a white-domed *marábout*, the resting-place of a Muhammedan saint,* rises among them. Not unlike Tenedos in the Ægean is this city of Tarabolos Gharb, though Tenedos lacks the Mesheyah groves of graceful Nakhil.

At last we let go our anchor, while seventeen boats full of screaming, yelling Tripolitans, Maltese, and Italians surrounded us, waiting eagerly for "pratique" to be declared, hoping then to carry us off in their strange craft to the Custom House.

Tarabolos Gharb, or Tripoli in the West, is so named in contradistinction to Trablous Shark, the Saracenic or Eastern Tripoli. Unfortunate mistakes have been made as to the two Tripolis. A houseful of furniture was once delivered at the Syrian Trablous, when it should have arrived in Africa.

Tripolis originally was the name for a country rather than a town. As Decapolis was the region of ten cities, Pentapolis of five, so Tripolis included within its limits three cities—Leptis, Sabrata, and Œa. It is upon the site of the last that Tarabolos Gharb now stands.†

Tripoli still is the name for the country as well as of its capital. The Vilayet of Tripoli is subject to the Sublime Porte, who appoints its Governor-

---

* The word *Marâbout* is used in North Africa both for the man and for his tomb. A Marâbout is a Dervish, Santon, or Muhammedan holy personage, often deficient in the brain power.

† There is a useful little sketch of the history of Tripoli in "The Country of the Moors" (chap. ii.).

general, occupies the country with ten thousand Turkish troops, and manipulates its revenue.

Tripoli comprises also the states of Fezzan and Barca. Fezzan stretches far away into the interior of Africa, while Barca, containing the ancient Cyrene, reaches even to the land of Egypt.

Tripoli is the most African and the most thoroughly Oriental of any town upon the north coast of Africa. Algeria and Tunisia are all more or less affected by French civilization, but the Tripoli of to-day is the Tripoli of Consul Tully's time, unchanging while all around has changed.

The finest groves of palm trees to be seen perhaps in the world surround Tarabolos Gharb, and stretch for scores of miles along the Mesheyah. These palms are a great feature in the Tripolitan scenery. The Sahara, the great African desert, rolls within a few miles of the city gates, its fine sand often whirling down upon the houses and penetrating everywhere.

Tripoli has always been a favourite point for the departure of great travellers for the interior, being nearly three hundred miles farther south than any more western port. From Ain Zhara, the first oasis beyond the Mesheyah, Barth, Nachtigal, the ill-fated Miss Tinne, and many other famous explorers, have set off to penetrate the Dark Continent.

From the British Consulate were waving all the flags available, among which the old Union Jack was very conspicuous. It was the Queen's birthday, and from courtesy national flags were hoisted on all the other consulates.

With our luggage around us we pulled over the blue waves, the Arab boatmen rousing in us some speculation as to their combination costumes, the difficulty being to decide which, amidst so many patches, was the original texture. So through the strange Levantine vessels we steered for the white quay in front of the Custom House, where there was gathered a strange crowd of Muhammedan Africans.

Amid Tripolitans of every hue, I managed to get to the Custom House, and successfully passed the luggage through the brown hands of the adhesive officials, having gravely exhibited my passport upside down to an intelligent official of the Ottoman Government.

"Yonder is Mr. Grace;" and an Englishman of military appearance came forward. To him I introduced myself, and in his company was soon on the way to the Tripolitan hostelry kept by a Maltese. Thence under the flying buttresses of some strange streets to deliver my letters of introduction, and among others to Mr. F. R. Drummond-Hay, H.B.M.'s Consul-general.

One of the first objects which met my gaze in the tortuous Tripolitan streets was the Quadrifrontal Roman arch so thoroughly described in Lyon Playfair's "Travels in the Footsteps of Bruce." * What

* Bruce left an elaborate series of drawings of this arch,

degradation! It is turned into a Maltese wine store, being built up at each opening with stone and plaster, and a glass window in the centre. To what base uses do we come!

> "Imperial Cæsar, dead and turned to clay,
> Might stop a hole to keep the wind away."

We entered and found the stonework perfect within, though both externally and internally the noble arch has lost much of its dignity by being one-third sunken in the ground, covered up by the rubbish of centuries. It is domed inside and the stones floriated. Outside are bas-relief trophies of Roman armour, and the remains of the figure of Victory in a leopard-drawn car. It was erected to the honour of Aurelius Antoninus and Lucius Aurelius Verus by one C. C. Celsus, manager of the public games.*

A ceaseless procession sweeps ever past Celsus'

---

two of which have been given in Colonel Playfair's work. The description in "The Country of the Moors" is most thorough and exhaustive. There are only three quadrifrontal arches in the world, the others being that of Caracalla at Tebessa, and Janus Quadrifrons at Rome.

* Mr. Rae gives the inscription and a translation of the same. I quote the latter. "To the Emperor Cæsar Aurelius Antoninus Augustus, Father of his Country, and to the Emperor Cæsar Lucius Aurelius Verus Armeniacus Augustus, Servius Scipio Orfitus proconsul, with Uttedius (?) Marcellus, his Lieutenant, dedicated: Caius Calpurnius Celsus, manager of the public games, Curator, Quinquennial Duumvir, and Flamen of Quirinus for life, made the arch in solid marble" ("Country of the Moors," p. 70).

SCENE IN BAZAAR. THE STORY-TELLER.

arch, a crowd which is not very different from that which looked upon it when that marble was newly chiselled—Arabs in their white *baracans*, picturesquely thrown round them, brown hairy camels growling and grunting as they bear their huge burdens, black negroes from the Soudân in native costume, and Africans of all shades and varieties.

Through open doors in some streets you may see in the gloom of the darkened interior, mills for grinding corn, where the blindfolded camel goes round and round on a never-ending circuit. A little bell is kept ringing by the *djmil's* circumambulations, and when he stops to think and chew the cud of contemplation, his sleeping driver wakes up and comes down from his shelf to "lubricate the machine." He winds it up with a useful stick, at which the camel gives a growl of protestation and moves on.

Bakeries are very common along the streets. The bun-like little loaves are extracted from the long oven on a shovel. The "coloured" bakers are nearly all from Fezzan (some thirty days' journey into the interior), where the heat is intense. They are negroes with woolly hair, and very dark skins, varying from chocolate to coal black.

In Tripoli you cannot go four paces without meeting negroes from the interior—Ghadamis, Mourzoukis, and sometimes even a Twarig. It seems as if about one-fifth of the population is black; and handsome men and women many of them are.

D

The other inhabitants are either Moslems or Jews. The Jews, however, are quite different to the Hebrews that we meet at home. To Europeans these African Jews appear identical with their Arab countrymen. In physiognomy the men often seem very little different. In their dress, however, to one who lives among them there is sufficient distinction. The Jew always wears something blue around his fez, or something with blue in it. But the Jews here have superstitious customs which would not be tolerated among their brethren in England.

Walking in the narrow streets of Tripoli one finds one's self in a new world, and yet a very old world, the surroundings are so utterly strange and yet all so thoroughly in keeping. At every step one is filled with a desire to preserve each peculiar scene in one's mind's eye for ever, for one is continually beholding some perfect Oriental picture which, by its brilliancy and quaint surroundings, would delight those at home if made permanent by the artist's hand.

Look* at that old *Marábout*, or Muhammedan saint, sitting yonder in the street, with his grizzled beard and his red and white turban, his beads in his hand, and a dirty *baracan* around him. At the time of the Aïssaouia festival a word from him might bring instant

---

* Many sentences in these sketches will be found to be in the present tense ; for they were written down as they now stand at the time. The author trusts that this may condone for an offence he feels guilty of—sudden transition from the past to the present, and *vice versâ*.

destruction to us, and cause the Arabs to fly upon us promptly with "Death to the infidel."

Come into one of the bazaars with us and sit near the Djâma 'l Shaib el Ain, the mosque built by the Saint of the Grey Eyes. Overhead lattice-work from one roof to another is covered by the delicate leaves of the vine, through which the bright sunlight percolates, tinged a delicious emerald green.

We sip our Arab coffee from tiny cups, each cupful separately made on the charcoal fire in a little tin measure with a long handle. Look at the moving panorama that sweeps by. One could never tire of watching it. Here comes a self-satisfied camel, looking down contemptuously alike on infidels, Jews, and sons of the faithful. He moves along with solemn gait and far-stretching neck, and woe betide you if you do not get out of his way. He passes away ever grumbling, as if he of all beasts in creation was the worst used and had most right to complain. Opposite to us two Turkish soldiers keep guard at the entrance to their barracks, and present arms with a clash as officers pass in and out.

A lieutenant in the Turkish cavalry joins us. He is dressed in dark blue clothes and red fez, his sword clashing at his side; a pleasant young fellow, banished from Constantinople because he will not obey his father, and marry a Turkish *houri* who has no charms for him. He has our sympathy at once. Nedjih Beki Bey is about eighteen years old, and greets us with a hearty grasp of the hand. He has been brought up in France, and speaks Parisian French. We saw a good deal of him at Tripoli, though his superior officers do not quite approve of his friendliness with Europeans. Nedjih inscribed his name one day in my birthday book in Turkish.

Here come sixteen Hammals, bearing a huge hogshead of sugar slung below four long poles. At each end of the poles are two of these porters, who all shuffle along in step, with their bare feet and ragged dress, chattering merrily, and all in good temper. Look at yonder African striding through the crowd as if the whole of Tripoli was his own; head erect and arms swinging. He is a Cavasse from one of the consulates, a Dragoman, black as ebony, his fine figure enveloped in a graceful and bright dress.

Here is a black woman, with frizzy curls, a basket on her head, a bright-coloured dress enveloping part of her dark figure, her face good-tempered, and the bright white teeth often exhibited merrily. So the crowds move on; we sip our coffee, and picturesque Moors on the divan smoke their *nârghilehs*, *chibouques*, or cigarettes; the bright sunlight streams down through the green leaves, the air resounds with Oriental shouts, buyer and seller vociferate, and piercing street cries come from many a strong throat.

All day long one felt that one was being rapidly Orientalized by these strange surroundings. But if one's surroundings in Tripoli were strange during the day-time, the weird scenes of the night were really startling. I had lain down in my African chamber (with a hole in the roof through which one saw the stars), and, after a day of sight-seeing, was dreaming of *Marábouts*, and of the members of the *Aïssaouia* going through the city with their drums, and singing the *Tekbir*. They were, I thought in my dreams, going to and fro proclaiming a *Jihad*, a holy war of extermination, against the infidels, and were about to wreak summary vengeance upon the first Christian they could find. They were even now on their way to the Locanda, where they had heard that a *Roumi* from the "land in the sea" had arrived. Louder and louder grew their wailing discordant song, while the drum in measured stroke accompanied the roar that came from the iron throats of hundreds of Arabs.

A cold perspiration broke out on my face when I began to realize that I was not asleep, but wide awake. I was alone, and it was about two in the morning, but the howls and the beating of the drum were *real!* There was no mistake—I was wide awake, and the noise was every instant growing louder. Hurriedly putting on some clothes, I felt my way in the darkness through the large room on to which mine opened, and again into an ante-chamber looking on to the street. On the floor of this room lay a negro, wrapped in his *baracan*. I did not know at the moment who or what he was, but stepping over him with my bare feet, I made my way to the window and looked into the roadway below.

Down the long narrow street, with its flying buttress-arches, was a blaze of light moving onwards from the distance. Several hundred Arabs waving torches and lanterns were marching with measured step and chanting an unearthly song, taken up by a single voice and then by the whole crowd. Many were leaping in their white *baracans*, flying like cats at the walls, as if to reach the upper story, and the crowd, which was entirely composed of men, completely filled the street.

They swept on towards the lattice where I stood, the waving lights illuminating the white houses, and the long wailing chorus sending a thrill through me. And what was it all? It was a marriage procession, upon the last night of the week's festivities; the bridegroom was being escorted to his bride. As the crowd advanced I saw an open space in which was the bridegroom supported by two friends. Lanterns were held towards him in order that all might behold. He looked very timid, and as if he did not at all like it, and seemed to be about eighteen or twenty years of age. The strange crowd surged past as they followed him, making the street echo to their strange song. They passed under a deep archway underneath some houses built over the street, and the noise gradually died away in the distance.

In the Land of the Mughreb* we were often brought face to face with scenes only half realized before, and here was one which was a vivid commentary on Matt. xxv. 5, 6—"While the bridegroom "tarried, they all slumbered and slept. And at mid-"night there was a cry made, Behold, the bridegroom "cometh ; go ye out to meet him."

* All North Africa was called the 'Country of the Sunset' (*Mughreb*) by the Mussulman conquerors from Arabia and the East.

CHAPTER V.

THE CHIEF MOSQUE OF TRIPOLI.

Muhammedan prejudices—Not easily overcome—Mosque of Gordji—Interior—The *Mihráb*—The *Kibleh* of Islam—The *Membar*—Ascend the *Minar*—The *Adzán* or cry of the Mueddin—Bird's-eye view of Tripoli—Backsheesh.

A SHOW of force is advisable, as well as the power of the golden key, if one would penetrate the sanctuaries of Islam at Tripoli.

His Excellency Achmet Rassim Pasha was good enough not only to give the Christian *Imaum* permission to enter the mosques, but directions came from the Borj for an escort to protect us if necessary. The dark lowering brows and gleaming teeth of the loiterers around the entrance of the Djâmas* were not reassuring, nor were they meant to be. Their horror at the desecration of that which is *'harram* (sacred) was scarcely overcome by a liberal distribution of the *Roumi's* piastres, or by the special inter-

---

* "A 'Jami' is a place where people assemble to pray—a house of public worship. A 'Masjid' is any place of prayer, private or public. From 'Masjid' we derive our mosque." (Burton.)

vention of the all-powerful *mahhboob*. But with a Cavasse from the consulate, a Zapti from the Kasbah, and the son of the Moslem trustee of the mosque property in Tripoli, we were fairly safe. The Emir also accompanied us.

We calculated our time so as not to arrive at the hour of prayer, and, taking the precaution of leaving our strong boots behind, we "slippered" along the narrow streets to the Djâma 'l Gordji, near to the British consulate, the most beautiful though the most modern of the Tripolitan mosques. Passing quickly through a gathering of angry faces we entered the Djâma, putting our shoes from off our feet, for the ground whereon we stood was holy. Quietly we trod the rich Turkish carpets, and asked our questions in subdued tones, creating much uneasiness in the minds of the guardian of the holy place by the numerous notes we made.

As all mosques are built on one general plan, it may be well to describe what is always seen, whether it is in the magnificent Santa Sophia at Stamboul, or in the awful Djâma 'l Kebir at Kairwân the Holy.

Corresponding in a slight degree to the chancel of our English churches is a small apse, very small indeed, called the *Mihrâb*. It is merely a niche in which the priest, the *Imaum*, stands with his face towards the *Kaába* of Mecca as he leads the prayers of the Faithful. This niche is always seen in the same place, in the centre of that wall which faces the Prophet's birthplace.

Towards the sacred black stone of Mecca (the *Hajar el Aswad*) all the worship of the Muhammedan is offered, and this is the only tendency to idolatry I know of in a faith which prohibits the likeness of anything which is in heaven above or in the earth beneath. Muhammed the Prophet first made Jerusalem the *Kibleh*, or spot towards which prayers were to be said, and this he did that he might attract the Jews; but failing in his purpose he changed the *Kibleh* to the *Bayt-Allah*, or "House of God" at Mecca, originally the pagan temple of the Arabs. "Turn thy face towards the holy temple of Mecca, and whenever ye pray turn your faces towards that place." So says the Korân (Sura ii. 129). Behind the *Imaum* kneel in rows the silent worshippers, or standing in their flowing robes hearken on Friday to the *Khâtbah*, the public official prayers, and loyal exhortations of the preacher addressing them from the *Membar*. The *Membar* (or pulpit) is always on the right side of the *Mihrâb;* its floor is twelve or fourteen feet above the level of the mosque, a flight of about twenty steps leading up to the spot where the *Khâtib* or preacher stands.

The interior of the mosque (or to speak more correctly the prayer chamber) is square or oblong, with a colonnade supporting the galleries and roof, and often over the main entrance a gallery-porch upon which stands the responsive choir, who chant verses of the Korân in a weird thrilling fashion. The mosque which we are now visiting was built by a Mameluke called El Hadji Muhammed Gordji. He lies in a mausoleum behind the prayer chamber. Adjoining his tomb is a quadrangle whose small chambers are inhabited by attendants and religious *attachés* of the mosque, after the fashion of almshouses. These devout Moslems of the Mosque all came in for a share in spoiling the *Roumi*.

After inspecting everything on the ground floor, we astonished the mosque-guardian by saying we were going to mount the *Minar*, or great tower, to obtain a bird's-eye view of the city of Tripoli. My Cavasse declined, upon the ground that it would make him giddy; he preferred to remain below and guard the door. So the Emir and I trotted up the tower. Round and round, up and up, now and then passing a loop-hole, which gave a momentary glimpse of white roofs and blue sea; then again we stumbled into darkness until certain muscles began to ache and we became hotter and more breathless. Near the top, the walls of the *Minar* are hung on the inside with the lamps used at the feast of Beiram after the Ramadan fast. They are used then to decorate the exterior of the *Minar* at night. It was inconsiderate of them to leave their dirty oily lamps for us to rub against in the dark.

At last we emerged into the dazzling blaze of

sunlight, and stood where the Mueddin appears five times a day as he cries over the city in prolonged wailing semi-tones—

"*Allahu ekbar*
"*Eshchedu ellē ilehe ellè allah*
"*Eshchedu enne Muhammed rasūl allah*
"*Heia alā ssalet*
"*Heia ala lfelah*
"*Allahu ekbar*
"*Le illeha ellè allah.*"

Adding in the evening and at night
"*Es sallè kheir min en nûm.*" *

Very few Europeans † have ascended this Minaret, where, as one walks round the balcony, one feels as if one was suspended in a captive balloon. The Emir said it made him feel rather uncomfortable to look over, and if I had not had a weakness for sitting on the upper topsail yard I might have been influenced also.

To describe such a scene adequately would be almost impossible, but I will endeavour to give my impressions as I leaned over the sides of the white stone car.

* See page 172 for the English of the *Adzân*. This is the Tunisian pronunciation of the identical words which are used every day from Morocco to India. They were taken down from the lips of a Sfaxine Muhammedan.

† Burton says, "A stranger must be careful how he appears at a minaret window, unless he would have a bullet whizzing past his head. Arabs are especially jealous of being over-looked, and have no fellow-feeling for votaries of 'beautiful views.'"

Right down below me lay the Oriental city of Tarabolos Gharb, a strange assortment of white buildings bordered by the blue waves of the Mediterranean, beating on dark chocolate rocks.

In an Eastern scene you cannot fail to be reminded first of all of the sun and its power, especially in summer-time. Glaring white were the flat roofs below, all of them varying in height. On one we saw women spreading out their clothes to dry. They need not leave them, for in five minutes the sun did its work, and they would be as dry as tinder. Down in the narrow streets were the ever-moving crowds of Tripolitans, negroes, *hammals* and Turkish soldiers; while a strange confusion of cries was borne up to us from buyers and sellers. Right below us four camels, as small as those in a Noah's ark, stood or knelt outside an oil mill, the sound of whose tinkling bell came up to us as the *djmil* patiently revolved within and crushed the olives.

The Emir pointed out to me all the well-known places of interest, especially the various consulates, and Mr. Drummond-Hay's residence close to us. Out on the blue waves the Turkish men-of-war and smaller vessels lay under the shelter of the line of rocks which juts out into the sea and nearly forms a natural harbour. It was proposed to connect these somewhat dangerous rocks and build them up into a pier, but a Pasha decided that "they were too old to bear the weight."

Towards the east, the palm groves extended as far as the eye could reach, parallel with the shore, while inland the Gharian hills appeared faintly over the hot desert. From the irregular buildings of the *Kashbah* on the east to the lighthouse on the west, from the Bab-el-Bahhr by the sea to the Bab-el-Yahoodi (the Jew's gate) behind us, all was dazzling white. Snowy domes and cupolas, or creamy roofs, some high, some low, courtyards with fountains playing, and half a dozen minarets, everything girded about and inclosed by the crenellated walls which abruptly end the town; for with the walls the city suddenly terminates, and the country begins. To the south, a mile or so beyond the gate, is the Jewish burying-place; to the east, two miles away, under the palms near the blue sea, is our English cemetery; and scattered here and there, ruined burying-places of the Muhammedans.

We were scarcely conscious of the length of time we remained on the top of the *Minar*, creating possibly a tendency to impatience in our escort below. We found the crowd considerably augmented by the prospect of "backsheesh," and looking alternately pleased and fanatically disgusted as the spoil was divided amongst them. Free and open mosques would be duly appreciated by the enterprising traveller.

Of the other mosques more anon.

CHAPTER VI.

THE ESPARTO MARKET.

The Souk-el-Halfa—Camel's vocal organs—Riding a *djmil*—Rising superior—The ship of the desert—*Mal-de-mer*—Sorting esparto—Coloured ladies and gentlemen—Fifty-seven okes—El Ghrad—Cameline trot—Grateful Bedouin.

THE 'Halfa,' or esparto grass, so much used in the manufacture of paper and the making of mats, is one of the chief exports of North Africa, being brought from the interior and carried to the coast on camel-back, frequently for immense distances.*

The Esparto market at Tripoli is a huge open-air quadrangle of about eight acres, surrounded by a high white wall, over which we can see the waving date palms, while within it is simply a desert of sand, burning hot under a scorching sun.

To-day the great enclosure is filled with yelling Arabs and screaming, groaning camels; for about eight hundred "nets" are in the market, each netful of esparto representing a camel load. This should weigh

---

* The Wady Halfa, or "Esparto Valley," on the Nile is a name familiar to newspaper readers.

about four hundredweight, but the Arabs often load the poor grumbling beasts up to eight or nine hundredweight. A roar goes up from the great enclosure, partly from the Arabs, but chiefly from the throats of the dissatisfied camels. The *djmil* never tires of giving vent to his feelings, the older ones in a hoarse roar or vindictive scream of passion, the younger ones with a calf-like bleat, at times very like a human voice inquiring for lactic refreshment. It is not easy to see the derivation of our English word camel. Yet take the Arabic plural *djmel* and soften it until you get *zmel*, then take our word and place a cedilla under the ç, putting the accent or emphasis upon the second syllable. Now notice the progressive connection çamél = smell = zmel = djmel. Perhaps, however, my etymology, like the camel's trot, is somewhat shaky.

Look at this great beast coming towards us, turning his head slowly from side to side, to see, perhaps, where his master intends to inflict the next "whack" with that stick he carries. He is to be my steed, and is to bear me some distance over the burning sands. But let him wait until I am ready; let him roast himself in the sun while we sip our *café à l'Arabe* in a little hut erected in the corner of the market for the use of European merchants. The inside of this summer-house erection is garnished with flaming cartoons, from the Italian *Punchinello*, bearing chiefly upon the political situation in the Levant.

Here we sit and watch the animated scene before us, as net after net is brought up to the steel-yard and weighed, the moist negroes pressing on the long lever beam to lift the esparto clear of the ground. Around this primitive machine is concentrated the greatest excitement, as the Arabs dispute violently over the weight and price.

My Bedouin smiles a grim ghastly smile as I prepare to climb on to the esparto mat that lies upon the *djmil's* back. But why should the brute grumble so much? Surely his theology is not sufficiently developed to enable him to nourish a secret hatred of the European *Imaum?*

It seems to be the camel's privilege to grumble on all occasions, as if no beast in creation was so badly used. At command of his driver, "*Nakh-nakh,*" the huge creature flops down on his knees, and squats upon the ground, that I may the more easily mount his back. Now comes one of the severe tests of camel riding—to hold on while he gains his feet. Up go his hind quarters half-way, his head still being down. Up come the bows on a level with the stern. Then with a mighty heave the huge quadruped gains his feet. If in the meantime you have not disappeared over his neck, or slid down his tail,—well, there you are, six or eight feet from the ground.

Now with long stride we push our way through the throng of growling camels and out at the gate of the esparto market. "*Dzarrh!*" yells the Bedouin, as, stick in hand, he tries to get a decent pace out of the *djmil.* Over the hot sands we go under the fierce sun, with a long easy step, up and down, up and down, the high lumpy back and the long neck undulating as he slowly plants his great cushioned feet on his native sand. We may realize from the long heaving motion one reason why the camel may be named "the ship of the desert." Woe betide any weak mortal who suffers from *mal de mer*, if he or she mounts a camel.

At last our journey is ended, as we find ourselves at the depôt where the *halfa* or *alpha* grass is sorted and compressed into iron-bound bales beneath a great lever. An hydraulic press is soon to take its place. One end of a huge beam is depressed by a perpendicular screw, worked by a dozen warm negroes in capstan fashion. The sons of Ham chatter merrily, and show their ivory teeth, as they go slowly round and round, apparently exerting all their strength. Round two piles of loose esparto in the yard are gathered negro men and women. The coloured gentlemen wear huge straw hats to protect their black complexions. They are engaged in pulling out any of the *halfa* which has a root attached. These they take to the women's group, where bronze Venuses, in strictly economical clothing, though bright and becoming, separate the roots from the grass.

In order to discover what effect the scorching sun had had upon my wasted form, I was weighed in the scales used for the *halfa*, and, sad to relate, found that my infidel person weighed fifty-seven okes. What an oke is it is only right for the credit of my relations to refrain from disclosure. The stately *djmil* once more rises from the ground with his burden of fifty-seven okes, groaning fearfully in consequence. Again with a "*Dzarrh!*" and a resounding application of the switch, we move off smartly over the hot sand.

One of the chief deterrents from camel exercise in Africa, is the presence of a monstrous insect amongst the hair, called a "*Ghrad.*" It is the shape and about the size of a domesticated cockroach, and this creature lives upon and fills itself to repletion with sanguineous fluid. We cannot wonder that camel-riding is not fashionable in Tripoli. Occasionally the camels are taken into the sea to be washed, but they resent such treatment as a personal insult.

As we rolled along I made a request in a weak moment for a trot. Goaded by his attendant into this most awful of paces, my *djmil* caused its much-jerked rider intense agony and internal misery for a "*mauvais cinq minutes,*" during which time I felt as if every portion of my frame was in the process of disintegration. Thenceforth I became resigned to a stately walk, feeling too that I had hurt the poor brute's sense of dignity by urging him to make an exhibition of himself.

Here we are again at the gate of the Souk el Halfa, and, in obedience to the word of command,

"*Nakh-nakh,*" my trusty steed tumbles down "all of a heap," pitching and rolling, until he finally settles in camel style on the sand. In this action a fresh illustration is seen of the ship-of-the-desert theory; for it was like striking suddenly upon a rock, then sliding off to settle down on the stony beach, beaten the while by the fierce waves. "May the *Roumi* come and ride upon his slave's *djmil* many days in each week," is the encouraging remark of the Bedouin, induced by an act of legerdemain in which coins mysteriously pass from sunburnt fingers into a chocolate-coloured palm. To this was added—

"Allah be praised. May thy countenance never grow cold."

The newly formed camel corps has all my deepest sympathy. I would give anything to see a charge.

CHAPTER VII.

WHITE FRIENDS AND BLACK.

The Maltese—British subjects—Our consulate at Tripoli—The French consul—Who is to have Tripoli?—Mysterious Italians—Walter Grace—Abdullah el Khartoumi—History of Miss Tinne—Her travels in Central Africa—Her tragic end—A visit to the home of Frederick—Parade of Turkish troops—Gratitude to the Sultan—Oriental band.

It would be only right now for me to introduce my Tripolitan friends and acquaintances, and to give some idea of the European colony in this city on the verge of the Sahara. Half a dozen families of English people at the outside are to be found in Tripoli, but there are hundreds of "British subjects" from that prolific island, Malta.

It is stated, and I believe quite correctly, that there are more Maltese living out of Malta than in it, though the Maltese islands are more densely populated than the same area in any part of the globe. The Maltese overflow the narrow limits of their island home, leaving at the same time some hundred and fifty thousand countrymen behind them in Malta and Gozo. Along the northern coast of Africa, they are to be found in every town in large numbers, a source of continual worry to our British consuls, whose protection they constantly seek. "British subjects" they claim to be on all occasions.

Some months ago England was startled by a telegram from Tunis informing us that an Englishman had been struck down by a French officer, and that the English consulate was surrounded by the British colony, who in crowds sought redress through H.M.'s consul, Mr. Reade.

Instead of the picture conveyed to most English minds of a bullying French officer abusing a harmless English traveller, the scene rising before my eyes was that of an insolent Maltese, conscious of British protection, behaving in an insulting way to some official at a time when relations between France and England were already strained. The Maltese in Alexandria also are a source of constant trouble to the English residents; they are always either starving or getting involved in disputes with the natives. Mr. F. R. Drummond Hay, the Consul-general, and Mr. Taylor, the Vice-consul, have their work cut out in tending their Maltese flock in Tarabolos Gharb.

The British consulate is one of the finest houses in Tripoli: a large, square, white edifice with flat roofs, surmounted by a tall flagstaff, upon which, on the day of my arrival, a considerable amount of gay bunting was displayed—a complete set of signal flags.

Let us enter the central courtyard, through a deep archway where the *cavasses* and attendants lounge. These gentlemen are worthy of notice in passing. Look at Muhammed yonder—a fine fellow, with his *sheshya* on the back of his shaven head; always has a smile for his superiors and a grim look for the troublesome inferiors. Then Mufta, in his clean, flowing robes, graceful and becoming—a most intelligent and even thoroughly honest dragoman. Just glance at that black youth, who stands by in white garments. He has suffered from a vindictive attack of small-pox, and looks as if small boys had shot pellets at his black visage while still impressionable. However, he tries to make amends by polishing his face beyond the verge of shininess.

Other picturesque Orientals lounge round the doorway or sit cross-legged within, and passing between these we enter a quadrangle, around which, with deep open galleries and verandahs, is built the house. In the centre of the court a fine *shumac* rises, casting a dark green shade on the white stones beneath. Golden bloom, bright and dazzling in the sunlight, is contrasted with the brilliant flowers of a handsome geranium, which is trained up the stem for some eight or ten feet. On the grand stone staircase are more gerania, and other bright flowers in pots, on either side.

The rooms are lofty, and well darkened from the fierce rays of the sun with mats, so that perfect coolness reigns within, when every one is scorched without.

British influence preponderates at Tripoli; chiefly, perhaps, because England has far the greatest share in her commerce. Then France, by her action in the adjoining province of Tunisia, has unmasked her spirit of annexation.

Monsieur Féraud, the French consul, is a cheerful, vivacious Algerian officer, who writes, and sketches, and paints by turns. I spent a most interesting afternoon with him, as he displayed his innumerable drawings in charcoal, and his brilliant views of Tripoli in *couleur de rose*.

He is writing a history of Tarabolos Gharb, and he will probably be able to show most excellent reasons for the annexation of Tripoli by his nation. He had the reputation of being a *consul de combat*,* but is anxious now to maintain a peaceful attitude.

Between Italy and France there exists the strongest jealousy as to the ultimate fate of Tripoli. The occupation of Tunis almost caused a proclamation of war between Rome and Paris, and the question now is, who is to have Tripoli?

The Porte naturally keeps a firm hold, and having more than trebled its soldiers in the pashalik, has no intention of backing out to please Gallican, Roman, or Briton.

* See Broadley's "Tunis, Past and Present."

The French say that troublesome tribes just hover on their border-land, and they will be obliged eventually to cross over into Tripoli to chastise them, and then the *chasse aux kroumirs* and the *promenade militaire* will be re-enacted.

Natives often favour British rule, as being the most just, as treating with the greatest respect the traditions of their country, and for commercial reasons, as being the only government which would bring prosperity.

Italy, within a stone's throw, naturally considers the prize should be hers. France has Algeria and Tunis, and England grasps the land of Egypt—why should she not possess Tripoli, with Fezzan and Barca, the connecting links in European Africa?

During my sojourn at Tripoli, I was somewhat puzzled by the movements of some Italian officers in mufti, who stayed at the Locanda with me. We were great friends, but they must excuse my saying that they were somewhat unfathomable. Why were they there, and in the pay of Italy, departing suddenly, returning unexpectedly? Though I had the pleasure of being kissed and of kissing my Italian friends on departure, after the manner and custom of their country, I was not quite satisfied as to the nature of their mission. They were charming fellows, nevertheless, though I anathematized them sometimes, when they would sing comic songs at midnight.

Mr. Walter Grace, one of my best friends in

Tripoli, has been nominated Roumelian consul, but the Porte is rather sore upon the subject, and does not, as yet, recognize his consular position. Not that they have anything against Mr. Grace, but Roumelia having been wrested from Turkey, the Sublime Porte is somewhat tardy in recognizing the new sovereignty. I was much indebted to this friend, for his continual efforts on my behalf during my sojourn in Tarabolos Gharb, and to Mrs. Grace, for the kindly hospitality so often extended to me.

At Mr. Grace's house I cultivated the acquaintance of one of his black servants, an Ethiopian of the deepest chocolate dye, "El Hadji Abdullah ben Said." He was born at Khartoum, some thirty years ago, and has been four times married. His first wife was a negress, the second an Egyptian of Cairo, the third an Algerine Moor, the fourth a Tripolitan.

Abdullah ("the servant of God") is a splendid fellow, well made and rather tall, with a pleasant countenance. He was full of most interesting information, having been servant, both to the ill-fated Miss Tinne, and to Captain Gill, who accompanied Professor Palmer into the Sinaitic desert.

He told me his whole life. How, when he was but a boy, he came down to the great city of Cairo, and how, when he was about fifteen, he met with Miss Tinne, who was travelling with her mother, and delighting to lead almost a nomad existence. He became thenceforth her servant, and with them travelled to Bongo, in Central Africa, and stayed there for two years, living in huts. Abdullah said that at Rek, where they were, the people were cannibals. Here Madame Tinne died, and also two female Dutch servants. From Rek they journeyed once more to the land of Egypt, and then returned to Khartoum, where Abdullah visited his old home. At Berber they lived for two months in tents. Thence they crossed the desert plains to Souakim, where they stayed for a month. They sailed over to the opposite shores, to Jeddah, the seaport of Mecca the Holy, but did not visit the shrine of Islam.

After a few weeks' stay they turned their steps northwards, and for three years remained in Cairo. Leaving Egypt's capital they journeyed to Europe, visiting Italy and the Riviera. Abdullah saw strange sights in the Land of the Giaour, sights he will never forget.

Miss Tinne did not care to remain in Europe, and again they set off for Africa. Arriving at Algiers, great preparations were made for an extended journey into the Sahara-land of the interior. At this time the captain and crew of the Dutch vessel *Meeuw*, which she had bought for her voyages in the Mediterranean, were engaged to accompany them inland, and serve as a European body-guard to Miss Tinne.

It must have been a strange and picturesque sight to have stood by the old Moorish Bab el Zoun, and seen the caravan of the 'Roumi Princess' pass out:

one hundred and thirty-five camels, bearing water and provisions, tents and presents, and accompanied by quite a small regiment of attendants. Our friend Abdullah was elated with the importance of himself and his mistress, as they took their departure for the interior.

Journeying far beyond the Atlas range, they arrived at the independent city of Tuggurt, of which such an interesting account is given in Dr. Tristram's "Sahara" (p. 279). Eastward they travel, even to Souf, and then returning to Bonah,* at the eastern extremity of Algeria, they take ship to Tunis, and afterwards to Malta.

After a residence of three months in Valetta, once more Miss Tinne longs for her wandering life amid the "Sons of the Desert." Crossing over to Tripoli with Abdullah, accompanied by his wife and boy, they prepare for the expedition into the interior.

It was winter-time when the train of camels and Arabs passed out through the Bab el Mesheyah, through the palm groves and out on to the great Sahara.

That night they encamped under those palm trees, that seem so familiar to me, at the first oasis in the desert, Ain Zhara.† Here they stayed awhile, in order to test everything by camp life, and to gather

---

* Bonah is described in the last chapter of this book.

† See pp. 99–106, for an account of our visit to this oasis of Ain Zhara.

together their forces. Thirty-five camels, some with iron tanks on their backs to carry water, some with tents, some with *baracans*, beads, silk and other presents for the natives. Two European sailors accompanied Miss Tinne, also fifteen Arabs, and two Soudânis (Fourrah and Dangidobro, now living in Tripoli), besides Abdullah. There were also three Bedouin women and three black girls.

They move away at last from Ain Zhara towards those distant Gharian hills, journeying ever southwards. Miss Tinne's intention was to travel by Sokna and Mourzouk (or Mursuk, see map) to far distant Bornu, with its inland sea, Lake Chad, and thence eventually to Cairo. From Walfellah, by Borndjim, they pass through Sokna, Sabbah, Diminhint, Dzera, Oddoa ("to-morrow"), and arrive at last at Mourzouk.

From Mourzouk they roamed over the country round, from the eastern river (Wady Sharki) to the western river (Wady Gharbi), and here (at Knókkin) they stayed ten days. The chief of the fierce Twarig race, the dread of all travellers, native or European, met them by the Wady Gharbi and seemed conciliated by Miss Tinne's presents. One is certainly amazed at the extraordinary courage on the part of a woman in travelling amongst such notoriously savage tribes. She returned to Mourzouk, but soon leaving it again moved on to Bilberani. The darkskinned Twarigs again appear to escort her to Ghrât, a city never yet entered by a Christian.

At Barjuish, five days from Fezzan, in the heart of Africa, Miss Tinne encamped, after the last stage in her journey of life, in the midst of these Twarigs, Touarigs or *Tawáriks* (as Barth calls them).

Abdullah had meantime been sent north from Mourzouk to purchase camels, and had arrived at Tripoli. It was three months later that he was shocked and horrified to hear sad news of his mistress. It seems that some of these faithless Twarigs had arranged with Muhammed of Tunis (who was acting in Abdullah's place), and a few of the Arab servants, to take Miss Tinne's life, and to divide the spoil. Early on the morning of the first of August, 1869, these dark-skinned murderers came into the encampment, as they were preparing for a start, picked a quarrel with the attendants, and as Miss Tinne came out of her tent to restore order, cut her down. Overpowering the escort, they killed the sailors and carried off one of the women servants, Jasmina, as a slave.

On hearing of this, Abdullah set off at once for Fezzan, and here he met the other servants who had fled, and returned with them to Tripoli for the judicial inquiry into Miss Tinne's death, which lasted for six months, and resulted in the conviction of five prisoners. After a year the woman, who had been sold into captivity, was also ransomed and brought back. Abdullah Ben Said has been handsomely treated by the relatives of his mistress, and receives a substantial monthly pension from England, as do also Fourrah, Dangidobro, and Jasmina, the other three survivors of her Egyptian suite.

It was very interesting to hear this from the lips of one who had been an eye-witness of nearly all, and since my return Mr. Ernest Tinne has kindly corrected and verified this story of Miss Tinne's travels. No authentic account of Miss Tinne's travels has before appeared, and the splendid "Plantae Tinnuæ" alone perpetuates the wanderings in Central Africa of her who has been called "the Heroine of the White Nile."

In 1871, Abdullah set off to accomplish the great religious act of a Muhammedan's life, the journey to Mecca and Medina.

> "Circling the sacred shrine in many a ring,
> He duly drank of Zemzem's holy spring,
> And kissed that stone, which white in heaven as snow,
> Doth now coal-black through breath of sinners show." *

He took with him his third wife, but she died on the way. He returns a *Hadji*, a duly certified pilgrim, having circumambulated the Kaaba, kissed the Hajar, and stoned El Shaitan.

Captain Gill, when travelling to Benghazi, took Abdullah with him. He was about to journey into the interior when his camels were seized by the Turkish Government, and his journey interrupted. In order to seek redress, Captain Gill went over to Constantinople, and on the outbreak of hostilities against Arabi Pasha, he proceeded to Cairo, and offered to

* Poems by Archbishop Trench.

assist Professor Palmer in his expedition to conciliate the Bedouins of the Sinaitic peninsula, and to purchase camels for transport. Abdullah had left his service, and did not go that fatal journey into the desert.

Abdullah has now settled down as head cook in Mr. Grace's establishment, and I can speak strongly in praise of his *cuisine*. He has a pleasant black face, and white teeth often displayed with great good nature. Strangely enough, he is not only a *Hadji*, but also a member of the confraternity of the *Aïssaouia*, and on the *Marâbout* day rushes wildly about the streets, jerking his thick lock of hair about, eating prickly pears, etc.

One evening, Edward O'Grady and I rode out to the Hermitage, the residence of the late Frederic Warrington, a name which is like a household word among the Arabs and the blacks for many a hundred miles into the interior. "Frederic," as he is still called by them, was the friend alike of negro and Arab, and was treated by them as one of themselves. To his salutation "*Salaam Alicûm*" (Peace be with you), they would give the reply which a follower of the prophet only could expect, "*Alicûm Salem.*" To others are coldly spoken the words, "*Beni cadiqi salem*" (Peace to the sons of the faithful).

'Frederic' never held an official position in Tripoli, save as interpreter to the consulate, but his power was very great with the natives. His father before him was a consul of no ordinary power, who stood at the helm at Tripoli and was all-powerful at the Borj. The late Mr. Warrington was the friend and adviser of all the great travellers who passed into the interior from Tripoli. If Miss Tinne had been guided by his advice, and certainly if she had been protected by his presence, the Twarig murderers would never have dared to execute their dastardly plans.

The Hermitage, which was left by Mr. Warrington to his adopted son, Edward O'Grady, is romantically situated in a clearing amongst the palms, a couple of miles from Tripoli, and it is surrounded by gardens. In Mr. Warrington's lifetime there was a small negro village with beehive huts, in the grounds, its inhabitants happy in their life under the shadow of Frederic's house, but in the sunshine of his protection.

It was very interesting to sit in rooms where the greatest African travellers had conversed as they planned their routes through unknown lands, Barth, Rohlf, Nachtigal, and many another. Here were all their pictures, too, in the photographic album.

From the outlook on the roof, standing by the flagstaff, we had a lovely view over the blue Mediterranean, a picture framed in palm trees whose dark branches waved mournfully in the evening air. The sun had descended and the swift night was rushing up, as only it does in southern latitudes.

Having seen much that was deeply interesting, we

caught our donkeys and away we went towards Tripoli in the darkness, avoiding the dreadful holes in the track. Crash! went the Emir, as his steed came down unexpectedly; but fortunately he was not hurt. It was a warning, however, to sit well back—*à l'Arabe*—near the tail.

Now down on the seashore, where, passing round a rocky promontory, the donkeys had to wade through the waves—a weird sensation in the darkness, yet I followed the Emir, and we safely emerged on to dry ground in Tripoli bay.

Each evening, about sunset, the troops march out upon the sand here, and, drawn up in line, give cheers for the Sultan, and return thanks for their food, clothes, and pay, as the bugle gives the signal for gratitude. It is a strange sight, and suggestively ironical, when one looks upon their awful clothes, and is told that their pay is hopelessly in arrear.*

In front of the general's house the band plays. They have begun to imitate European music, but the result is as trying to the infidel European as it is unsatisfactory to the drum-loving son of the faithful. The conductor turns his back upon the band in order that he may not present it to the General. Two men are solely employed in twirling round pagoda-like edifices on poles, with innumerable bells attached, while others blow trumpets in the German band style.

When a European orchestra first appeared at

* See extract from letter at end of chapter.

Stamboul and played before the Sultan, his Ottoman Majesty with his court sat to hear the performance. "A ♮" was struck by some one with a tuning-fork, and every instrument in the band began to tune up or flatten down to concert pitch. Violins scraped, hautboys piped, bassoons grunted, trumpets sounded, and trombones bellowed. There was a pause. The conductor struck his desk; but the performance was stopped by a strong voice from the imperial box. It was the Sultan, who roared, "Let the dogs play that tune again." To his Oriental ear nothing was so delightful as the tuning up.

Extract from Letter to the Author.

"With regard to the number of soldiers here in "Tripoli, it is impossible to get from the authorities "exact statements, and they are very unwilling to give "any information on this point. For myself, I think "we have about five thousand men stationed in and "around Tripoli. More than half of these are supplied "with Martini-Henry rifles, the remainder with Snider. "The cavalry, some four hundred horse, are supplied "with the Winchester repeating rifle, containing sixteen "charges. There is a battery of horse artillery (very "well mounted), of sixteen Armstrong breech-loading "guns, with all equipments first rate.

"There are three new earthwork forts to the west-"ward of the town, one south-east, one east, one com-"manding the entrance to the harbour just eastward "of the buoys, and one up by the lighthouse. The "soldiers, cavalry, artillery, and forts, have all been "instituted since the French excitement in Tunis.

"Formerly there were some three thousand men in "the whole pashalik, but now some eight thousand five "hundred all told. The regiments are numerous, but "not fully up to strength, even rather under, four hun-"dred men each battalion. Discipline very bad, officers "seeming to have no *esprit de corps;* and the men "being so badly paid are not proud of wearing his "Majesty's uniform (rags). They are fed plentifully "but poorly, and paid one month's wages in every "six, when they are lucky."

CHAPTER VIII.

EL SOUK EL DJAMA (THE FRIDAY FAIR).

The Tuesday fair and the Friday fair—Off to Am Roos—Youthful piety—Fiery steed—Barb and *djmil* in collision—The Mesheyan oasis—Baracans and how to use them—The fair—Haggling—*Black*smiths—Bellows—Pepper—Sneezes—*Mishmash*—Camelette—Sheep-slaughter—Native music—Hath not charms—Am Roos—Arab interior—*Legmi*—Its awful effects.

Two Moorish markets are held each week outside the town of Tripoli.

Beyond the Bab el Hundouk (or Fondouk) a huge and noisy gathering of Berbers, Bedouins, donkeys, Moors, and camels spreads itself out over the hot sand on the shore. The strange crowd, so picturesque and bright, reaches even to the blue wavelets of the Mediterranean as they curl over under this burning sun. This is the Tuesday fair, the Souk el Thelath. On the Muhammedan Sabbath, and early in the morning, another "Souk" is held some distance away, in the palm groves of the *Mesheyah*, the great oasis which separates Tripoli from the Sahara.

This Souk el Djâma, or Friday Fair, is to be found near the quaint little village of Am Roos, some five miles or so from the white walls of Tripoli. Thither we rode early one Friday morning, Mr. Grace and our Italian friends in one of the Maltese *buggies*, the former having kindly placed his Arab steed at my disposal in order that I might have more freedom of action. My friend the Emir was also upon a spirited barb, which seemed anxious to maintain the character bestowed upon these fleet steeds of Barbary.

Gently we ambled through the crowded bazaars, a youthful *Marâbout* blowing out his cheeks at us, and then slapping them, to produce the paper-bag-explosion effect. This was indicative of hatred and disgust for the *Roumi*. He was an idiot. Allah had transferred a portion of his reason beforehand to Paradise, and therefore he was a Saint. Past the Kasbah, and then between the Turkish guards at the Bab el Mesheyah. Under the archway and out on to the burning sands, where the camels were reclining in their hundreds, as they are ever wont, hoppled by a tight cord round both shin and thigh-bone, so that they cannot easily rise from a kneeling position, and if they do rise cannot get away. My Arab steed here took a mean advantage of my kind nature and promptly bolted over the sands, through the camels and negroes and donkeys and Bedouins; but as he inflicted no personal injury upon any one, it was rather refreshing than otherwise. I had been told that the curb was superfluous, and the snaffle only necessary, but found this was a mistake, as I flew through the air on

"My Arab shod with fire."

I soon brought the Gazelle to, however, and we thenceforth maintained a mutual understanding.

Less fortunate was a young Swiss friend a week or two before. His fiery barb had bolted along a narrow opening under the palms, and as he was wildly careering the road was suddenly blocked by a contemplative camel, who calmly emerged from a by-road and was solemnly stalking across the path down which this Helvetian Gilpin was tearing. The *djmil* was laden with stones. Like an express dashing into a goods train, so Wittstein's steed hurled itself into the camel's flank. The camel is notoriously a difficult creature to animate, but never did *djmil* move so briskly as after the collision, when our friend, performing several gyrations in mid-air, came down somewhere in the direction of the Soudân. Wittstein broke his arm, the camel broke into a trot. The stones flew in all directions, and the much-abused camel received a dreadful shock to its nerves from this sudden contact with an unbeliever. Its mind has ever since been quite warped and biassed with a severe prejudice against the Infidel in general, and a muzzle has become a necessary part of its outfit. Both horse and rider, however, were soon so far recovered as to be able to accompany us on another expedition a few days later.

This morning we have a delightful ride through the Mesheyan oasis. Palm trees on all sides, tall and graceful, bowing ever and anon in the breeze, or basking in the scorching sun, pomegranate bushes in abundance, with their crimson flowers, caroub trees with ripening pods, stately olives planted so regularly row after row in the olive-yards, broad-leafed banana, flaming oleander, gentle delicate orange bloom, flower and bush and tree alike, all lovely with a semi-tropical loveliness.

On all sides the white stone wings of the Beers, or wells, are seen, and the ever-creaking wheel as the patient ox descends an inclined plane drawing up the *dillu*, the great skin, full of water, which gushes out into the irrigating channels directing its course. Here is the secret of most of the loveliness around.

Strange-looking Bedouins pass us with their black burnt faces; some aloft on camels with the long *bindiggah*, the Arab gun, slung across their shoulders, some driving heavily laden asses almost hidden by their loads, the driver often perched upon the over-burdened donkey's back until one wonders what exquisite torture can induce the tiny quadruped to amble along so briskly.

The Moors and Arabs are all gracefully enveloped in the long white *baracan*, completely draping them, one end of its almost endless folds often flung over the *tarboosh* as an additional protection from the sun's fierce rays.

AN ARAB INTERIOR.

The black driver of the cart on springs in which our friends rode, was draped most artistically, and though he trotted alongside most of the way his graceful costume was never disarranged. This *baracan*, which is worn over the linen underclothing, is of prodigious size when completely opened out. I have seen it used for the sail on a barge, spread out upon the oars. It is used at night for bed and bedclothes, and after a ventilating and depopulating shake it is donned in the daytime as a protection against either heat or cold. It is, however, scarcely advisable to borrow a *baracan*. If you overcome the fanaticism of the Arab, and obtain his permission to envelop yourself in its folds, you have still the fanaticism of insect life to contend with, and it wages a merciless war upon the *Roumi*. Then a European never wears a *baracan* gracefully; he always looks either like a mummy revived, or an individual escaped from the cooling-room of a Turkish bath.

The sun rose higher and higher above the feathery palms and it was nearly nine a.m., when, after our hot ride through the *Mesheyah*, we emerged into the large "clearing" among the trees, where a perfect Babel of sounds assails our ears, and we see before us a confused crowd of savage-looking Orientals. A square of some two or three acres is filled from end to end with Moors and Bedouins, conducting business in that delightfully Oriental fashion which is known among us as "haggling." The wares are spread on the ground, and the Arab and his friends squat round them and gesticulate and shout and argue in a truly African manner, arms, hands, and shoulders talking just as much as the tongue.

Here are veritable *black*smiths hammering out small swords, and the anvil upon which they work is a camel's thigh-bone. Look at their bellows, not quite so comical as the *sapaghi*, the long boots of Southern Russia, which one has actually seen used for blowing up the *samovar*, yet equally strange, being made of an entire hairy goatskin. One of the feet is the nozzle, and a large opening in the skin is opened and shut suddenly so as to inflate the skin and discharge the air into the embers.

Why are all the Arabs over yonder sneezing in such a ridiculous manner? "In the name of the Prophet, red pepper beans." That is the reason; and as we approach we become equally ridiculous. Piles of red pepper beans are spread in front of the little booths, and the air is so impregnated that every living creature must of necessity sneeze, until tears of sincere grief trickle down one's cheeks; even the camels join in and explode at intervals. There is nothing more moving than to be near a camel when it sneezes.

In the centre of the fair ground is a large flat stone or rock upon which executions take place. The last time a wretched man was beheaded, the efforts of the executioner were for some time painfully unsuccessful, and the poor creature's mother was a witness of it all.

A more pleasant topic is *mishmash*, in which I indulged freely. For about a penny a large hatful of these delicious apricots could be purchased from the luscious piles around. An Arab probably would have received five times as much, but then we should have had to hire a donkey to carry them. As I ate the delicious fruit, doubly delicious under this scorching sun, I naturally threw down the stones on the sand. I was soon astonished by the sensation I created.

"In the Name of Allah, does the *Roumi* know what he does? Does he not know that the stone containeth a kernel, and that the kernel is sweet and good?"

The small boys with their bronze skins dived into the sand for the stones, and a regular scrimmage took place, though their elders looked on sternly and with lowering brows, as the children touched that which the infidel had defiled. I am told that apricots are sold often upon the understanding that the stones are returned after the *mishmash* has been consumed, the sweet kernel being so much valued.

In one corner of the *Souk*, camels were being bought and sold. I fell head over ears in love with a stately little camelette, about seven hands high, covered thickly with white downy hair. I might have her, the owner said, for twenty mahboobs, about £3 15s. How charming it would have been to have led her home to the 'North Countrie,' and introduced her to my Constantinopolitan pariah "Toure," * yet I'm afraid I could not have found an abundant supply of prickly pear for her under our grey skies.

What evil tempers camels have.† Even camels of tender years carry the disdainful air and the projecting under lip, ready always to pout or sneer, or snarl, or grumble, or, worse still, to bite. But never among the hundreds and hundreds of camels I was continually meeting, did I ever see one that charmed me so completely as this lovely little humpty-dumpty at El Souk el Djâma of Tripoli.

Sheep and goats are huddled together in yonder corner, frightened and trembling as the yelling Arabs rush in upon them and drag out, now a great black goat with curly horns, now a fat-tailed lopped-eared sheep, so different from our *Ovis Britannicus*. The tail appears as wide as the body (when covered by

---

* Since I first wrote these words poor Toure has met with an untimely end. I had picked him out of a nest in a narrow street in Stamboul, and brought him up from puppyhood, through youth to maturity, and had succeeded in civilizing him, when in a fight he died. Few dogs have been more regretted than Toure. He was a fine specimen of the Eastern dog, and his skin makes a handsome rug.

† It is said that Bedouins, through eating camel's flesh and drinking camel's milk, have become cruel and treacherous.

its wool), and hangs down thick and heavy, a huge lappet of prodigious weight.

The sand around is stained a deep crimson, from the massacre of the innocent sheep this morning, and on some bushes hang in the scorching sun skins that gaily trotted into the market a few hours ago. The Arabs in buying and selling seize upon some particular sheep, and drag it, despite its vigorous struggles, out of the flock. Then in turn they lift it to judge its weight. The fearful weight of splendid meat nearly breaks the seller's back, but the buyer finds it absurdly light, nothing but skin and bones.

Under the palm trees we find two African musicians, who have travelled from Fez in Morocco, the place which gives its name to the *sheshiya* of Tunis, the *tarboosh* of Tripoli, that thick bullet-proof skull-cap so invaluable in this country, where the bullet and the sun are almost equally powerful. The Morrocines were beguiled into playing for us, and they produced the most soul-creeping melodies that they were able to invent out of two notes on an African stringed instrument, the *gimbrih*, and a skin-covered drum called a *bindïr*. I was waiting patiently for them to begin, supposing in my simplicity that they were going through a species of preliminary tuning up; but they steadily adhered to the two notes, after the fashion of the Ethiopian serenader with the long boots. Imagine all the music you could extract from two adjoining notes on a piano, persistently played in alternation for some twenty minutes, and accompany the same with a stick upon the table, and you have true Oriental music.

We next prevailed upon the Morrocine with the *gimbrih* to sing in his own language. His song doubtless was of burning deserts and flying steeds, of sun-faced youths and star-eyed damsels, of love under difficulties, of war and the sword.

No doubt if I had been trained to appreciate Arabic music and African songs my heart would have thrilled with varying emotions. Yet, as it was, only one thrilled me, and that was a strong desire to go away somewhere; the same feeling that an ancient and decrepit barrel organ arouses in the breast of the unsympathetic Briton at home.

There sat the old Morrocine, with his dark face and white turban, twanging his two-stringed banjo; there sat likewise his brother in crime, for ever keeping up on his tambourine a "trumatee trum-trum, trum-atee-trum-trum;" there would they have been still sitting under the palm trees, and bringing discredit upon the neighbourhood, if we had not intervened and paid them to stop.

With more easy consciences we now wandered away from the crowd of shouting, gesticulating Arabs, through the palm groves and under the mulberry trees, until we saw before us the white houses of the village of Ain Roos.

The dwellings of the villagers here as elsewhere have no external windows, but are built round a small courtyard, into which all the rooms open. There is just one door opening into this courtyard from without.

One story high are all these houses in the country, and builded of a species of cement, composed of wet sand and stones tightly packed together within a temporary framework of boards, which boards are removed as the walls become dry and hard. Through such walls could "thieves dig through and steal."* Into a Moorish house we could never hope to enter—*that* a Muhammedan himself could scarcely expect; but we obtained access to the house of an Arab Jew named Messawad, in Am Roos, and explored the same from cellar to attic, to speak metaphorically where neither cellar nor attic exist.

Entering the enclosure, dazzling white, as the blazing sun beats down on the white cement floor, we see doors opening into various chambers around, some sleeping-rooms, one a guest-chamber, one a lumber-room and a hen-house, while steps lead up on to the flat roof and to a store built on one corner thereof. From the roof you might run along to the roof of another house without returning downstairs, and in large towns thus escape most easily in case of emergency. "Let him that is upon the house-top not return into the house to take anything out of his

* Matt. vi. 19 (Greek).

house."* This seems very natural to one here, as do so very many Bible expressions and incidents.

In a cool recess we sat cross-legged upon esparto matting, and sipped *legmi*, so acceptable after a few hours under this scorching sun, while the little dark-skinned children gathered round in amazement.

Legmi, the beverage of the Arabs, is a noble drink. The Arab climbs the date palm, and making an incision at the top fastens there an earthen jar, which collects the sap draining from this wound.

If not used the same day the *legmi* becomes very unpleasant and also intoxicating. Our *legmi*, however, was perfectly fresh. Most delicious I found it that scorching morning. In appearance like milk, but in taste somewhat like soda water after effervescence, and sweetened. This indeed is "The cup which cheers but does not inebriate."

Undoubtedly it "cheered" us, for we all felt happier and merrier after our *legmi*, and began to find much that was funny in the little village. The Emir excited the cocks of Am Roos by crowing magnificently; we persuaded ourselves into believing that a tumble-down dwelling we passed was a finer ruin than anything at Leptis Magna; while an aged Jewess was declared to be a splendid piece of antique Roman ware, and a patient donkey who gazed benignly upon us out of a door, wagging his ears as the flies crept in and out, excited cries of derision.

* Matt. xxiv. 17.

So we pass through the village, the inhabitants all at work on the shady side of the street, hammering, cobbling, and bargaining, but never a Moorish woman to be seen, nothing but men and boys.

It was nearly midday when the fleet-footed "Gazelle" brought me over the sands to the Bab el Mesheyah. The molten ball of fire, of which we know nothing in our humid island, was right over our heads, and small dark shadows circled just round our feet.

CHAPTER IX.

WITHIN AND WITHOUT THE WALLS OF TRIPOLI.

Infant schools—High school for Moors—Switches—Mosques—Tunisian refugees—Moslem pictures—*Rakaats*—Ablutions—Dragoot the Corsair—*Kuss-kuss-öo*—Arab Jews—Synagogues—Blood of Christian—The walls of Tripoli—View near lighthouse—Outside the walls—A *beer*—An odd trio—The ox and two asses—Extra-mural fair—Money-changing—The orange-blossom and mothers-in-law—Harêms.

I SHOULD imagine that school-life was somewhat monotonous in Tripoli. Escorted by Muphta and the Emir, I went one day to inspect the elementary education system of this country. After passing through tortuous by-streets, at last we heard in the distance a hum, then as we drew nearer, a steady roar, and arriving at last outside the building, the noise developed into a prolonged and vigorous shout.

Up a narrow staircase in single file, and pushing open the door, an awful and sudden silence fell upon the crowd of cross-legged children—a contrast indeed to the discordant Babel which had deafened one a moment before. In a little chamber, some ten yards square, were gathered seventy or eighty diminutive Moors, all sitting cross-legged upon the floor, some in turbans, some in *sheshyas*, some in coloured garments of a nondescript description, but nearly all of a very tender age, perhaps seven or eight.

In one corner, on a slightly raised dais, sat, also cross-legged, a very sullen, fanatical, middle-aged Moslem, with a long switch, teaching the young idea to shout. He glared fiercely at us for disturbing his school, and Muphta's polite assurances did not seem to soothe him at all. After introducing ourselves as most distinguished visitors we told him we should like the children to continue their lessons, which consisted in learning the alphabet in Arabic. With an overwhelming crash the lung-power of young Tripoli was ably demonstrated, as every child howled its loudest, swaying to and fro, and roaring out all the letters it knew.

Each little scholar who was slightly advanced had a circle of smaller children round him, whom he led in this letter exercise, declaiming one letter after another, which they echoed loudly, all swaying to and fro like little Chinese mandarins. We soon retired, salaaming to the sour-looking master and frightened-looking little Muhammedans as we backed out.

Another time we went to a school for children of riper years, a sort of "High School for Moors," which was held in a mosque-like building. Here we took off our shoes at the entrance, and made obeisance to the Head Master in his Cap and Gown. His cap, however, was a *sheshya;* his gown of white flowing material. He did not rise, and seemed rather to resent our intrusion. I walked round, looking over the boys' slates, or rather small black boards, upon which they wrote with chalk.

There was no furniture of any kind, save some mats upon the floor. The boys all squatted under the dome, and were certainly less noisy than in the first school. Elder scholars corrected the exercises of the younger boys, all of which were sentences from the Korân, which in Muhammedan countries forms the weft and woof of education. It has to be learnt off by heart, which being accomplished a Moslem education is almost complete.

The master had a magnificent switch, capable I am sure of awe-inspiring and resounding whacks. Unfortunately, I came away without seeing corporal punishment inflicted. An Eastern maxim which offers its consolation to him that is chastised declares that—

"The green rod is of the trees of Paradise."

We have yet three mosques to see, and now must pass through the bazaars to the Djáma Shaib el Ain, the mosque of the grey-eyed saint. In the courtyard here is gathered an immense number of Tunisians and Bedouins, who have fled from the French army and placed themselves under Tripoline protection.

Very destitute they seemed, dirty, wan, and hunger-bitten. As we passed they surged in a vociferating mass, crying out, holding up their hands. It was a distribution of bread that was taking place, and each one was rushing for a dole. One pitied these dark-skinned women and children, in a foreign land, driven from their homes in Tunisia by the stranger.

Our escort guarded us from insults as we entered the mosque. An old Moor at the door sorrowfully shook his head and moaned, "*Ach set la hâl*" (The world is changing). Yes, when infidels are escorted by the servants of a Moslem government, and bidden to enter the holy places, it is somewhat trying for the devout Moslem.

There is nothing attractive in the Djâma Shaib el Ain: a gaudily painted pulpit, pillars quite disfigured with coarse imitation marbling, and, strange sight to see in the Iconoclastic Dar el Islam! three prints, near the *mihrâb*—one of Mecca, with the Kaaba, the Bayt Allah; another of Medina, the resting-place of the Prophet; and the third of El Kûds, the Holy City (Jerusalem), with the mosque of Omar. This seems almost a contravention of the decree of Muhammed against all pictures.

We go to the Djâma Bashaw, or Pasha's mosque, so called from its founder, Achmet Pasha. This mosque comes second in the order of beauty in Tripoli. Rows of marble pillars support a roof in which are an immense number of small domes. Black and white tiles on the floor, and a delicately tinted dado of tiles round the walls to a considerable height; above it the lovely arabesque work in plaster of Paris.

Muhammedans were praying towards the *Kibleh* as we quietly passed round the square prayer-chamber, and they paid no attention to us, being absorbed in their devotions. First they stand, and lift up their hands with palms in front. Then, after a moment's prayer, they proceed to adoration, kneeling on the floor and prostrating until they touch the ground with their foreheads. Remaining upon their knees they pray for some time, now and again between their short prayers bending and kneeling in *rakaats*, or prostrations. Finally, the Moslem solemnly and slowly shakes his head and exclaims, "*Allah-ach-Kebar*" (God is most great).

Outside the mosque, in the courtyard, other Moslems were performing their ablutions, which they must go through always before prayer. If they are in the desert, where there is no water, fine sand is allowed to take its place. The ordinary ablution consists of washing the hands and arms to the elbows, the head and face, and the feet to the ankles, which ablutions are accompanied by short prayers.

One more mosque, that of the great Tripolitan corsair, Dragut, who perished at St. Elmo, in Malta, in the memorable siege of Valetta by the Moslems, when such magnificent bravery was shown by the knights of St. John. The interior of the mosque is hideously painted, or rather daubed, and it has no redeeming features; but the most interesting part is the *Marábout* of Sidi Dragut, where, under a white *Kouba*, lies that corsair, now powerless, whose name once brought terror to the whole Levant.

The black Muhammedan saint in charge of the mausoleum admitted us when he saw our escort, and passing in among numerous little tombs and yellow flags we entered the small chamber where Dragut the corsair lies after his wonderful career in the sixteenth century. Brought back from Malta, he is buried in his town of Tripoli, which he had wrested from its brave Christian defender, the knight De Valier.

In the governor's palace at Valetta you may see the sword, axe, and surtout of Dragut Reis, preserved amid the many interesting relics of that collection. To this *Marábout* of Sidi Dragut, which is quite separate from his mosque, facing the harbour and entered from the Marina, numbers of Moorish women come to pray, and talk over the characters of their Tripoline neighbours.

At our midday meal I was favoured with a dish of *Kuss-kuss-óo*, the *pièce de résistance* of North Africa, the very mention of which will bring a smile of pleasant recollection upon the Bedouin's grim visage. It is made of whole barley grain, steamed over the meat, and served with it in balls, or some strange shape, often like a Chinaman's hat. The only fault

I can find with this well-known African dish is that it satisfies in an untimely fashion.

I had worked the Emir too hard lately in sight-seeing, so I persuaded him to rest this afternoon, while I wandered on in the broiling sun. Through the Jews' quarter I found my way, peeping into several synagogues, where they were sweeping and preparing for the sabbath, and examining the ark and the rolls of the *Torah*, the *Nebiim*, and the *Cetubim*—not printed books, but real old scriptural rolls.

A good deal of excitement has been created in the Levant lately on the subject of the *Sangue Christiani*, the use of Christian blood in the Passover rites. It has been stated again and again that the Jews in the East, many of whom have fallen into depraved and superstitious customs, consider that their Passover sacrifice is not efficacious if there is not added to the lamb's blood sprinkled on lintel and doorpost, the *blood of a newly slain Christian!* Certain it is that children, and even grown-up persons, have mysteriously disappeared about Passover-time, and never been seen again. A recent convert from Judaism to Roman Catholicism has written a book on the subject, making startling revelations.

Passing through a busy Jewish market I wandered down to the north-western horn of this crescent city, and climbing up some ruins I did not find much difficulty in ascending to the top of the city wall, a little below the lighthouse. The view was picturesque and characteristic. On one side was the city, with its white flat-roofed houses, and great courtyards, in one of which close to me were camels munching prickly pear. Before me was the harbour, with the pier and fort,* its strange boats and boatmen in gay clothing pulling over the deep blue waters. Close beneath me, under the walls, was a desolate sea-shore stretching westwards, the fierce sun beating on chocolate-coloured rocks and lazy wavelets.

At last I became aware that a strange shouting, which had been going on for a few minutes, from a military individual with a gun farther up the walls, was meant for me. Evidently I had no business there, and ought to come down. To satisfy him I made a feint of descending, and disappeared behind a projection.

After a reasonable time had elapsed I looked out, and the sentinel was going the other way. In three minutes I had scrambled down the walls on to the seashore, and so had made an exit from Tripoli without using the gates. This had evidently been done before. I intended to encompass the city after walking a little along the harbour.

Some slight excavations were being made here, and, instead of wheelbarrows, small donkeys carried

* This fort is known among the Arabs as *El Bordj Bou Leilah*, or, "Fort of One Night," from a tradition that it miraculously arose between sunset and sunrise. It certainly appears to have been erected in the dark.

baskets full of earth in a continuous stream. Piles of earthenware near the pier were for sale—huge oil jars and small water jugs, pointed at the lower end. I often wanted to know why so much of the Oriental ware lacked a flat base upon which to stand, and since wandering in the deserts I imagine the solution is there to be found, and that it is because a pointed vessel will stand so much more firmly than a flat-bottomed one in the sand.

Setting out to walk round the walls I passed along the seashore, where an Arab was washing his clothes in a salt-water pool, and turning the corner, left the sea behind me. In the intense heat I moved inland towards the Bab el Djedid, more generally known as the Jews' Gate—Bab el Yahoodi. The walls are a great height here. White and glaring, they rise from a broad space, which at this corner I should imagine had been cleared intentionally, as the land seems nowadays to be higher beyond it, perhaps owing to *débris* from the city.

All alone, not a creature in sight, I sat down on a hot stone and watched the ants rushing about, while the sun glared down upon my fez, and fried my hands and face. Soon an urchin, peering over a mound at me, rushed off to bring his friends. I moved on, and left the small fry in their picturesque garments gazing in astonishment. Here is the Jews' Gate, and away a mile or so to the south-west the Jews' Cemetery.

Over the country are sprinkled white *beers* or *siniehs*—the former word being simply the generic term for well, so often occurring in our Bible (as Beer-sheba, etc.); the latter, *sinich*, describing the mode by which the water is brought up. I stood on the steps of one of the white *dellu*, the wing-like stone edifices between which the wheel works as the ox or camel, descending the inclined plane, hauls up a skin full of gushing water, which rushes over the land along any little channel into which it is diverted by the foot of the Arab. One is reminded of Moses' promise, that in Palestine the Israelites would no longer have to use such means of irrigation, for there would be plenty of rain. It was not to be as the land which they had left, "where," says he, "thou sowedst thy seed *and wateredst it with thy foot.*" *

Close to the *beer* was a large circle spread over with barley, and round and round moved a strange trio. An ox in the centre, from whose mouth hung pieces of barley stalk, as he enjoyed unmuzzled this treading out of corn.† To his horns a rope was attached, and then fastened round a donkey's neck, who moved alongside the ox, and still another donkey appendant on the outside of the circle. These all moved round and round, driven by a negro in white *sheshyah, seriyah* (long shirt), and *sirnwall* (loose trousers). He was followed by a chocolate youth with a rake, who moved the barley as the others passed over it.

* Deut. xi. 10.   † Deut. xxv. 4.

In my white flannels I stood for a moment on the steps of the *sinich*, and then innocently hopped down alongside the donkeys and ox. The latter had been so busy munching his corn that he had not seen the infidel before, and as I appeared in the midst, donkeys and ox simultaneously fled, the negroes chasing after them and shouting wildly. I sat down on the stone steps and laughed most unfeelingly to see the two young donkeys tearing away and dragging the poor old bullock by the horns. Eventually the swift-footed Soudânis secured the trio, and brought them back, using unchoice words. When, however, they saw me laughing, they joined in and laughed heartily, showing their brilliant white teeth good-naturedly.

Leaving my asinine friends, I passed the Bab el Djedid, and under the great walls moved on towards the Bab el Fondouk, by which you may enter the Bazaars, and outside of which was quite a fair going on, camels grunting, Arabs selling bread on trays, and a gathering of the strangest costumes mixed up in Oriental confusion. There were wild-looking Bedouins, Tripoline Moors, and many negroes, while Turkish soldiers passed hand in hand through the crowd. Here was a *fondouk*, or *caravanserai*, where the beasts of burden lay within a colonnaded enclosure, and their owners squatted under the shade, cooking their provisions. The fair was nearly over, as it was late in the afternoon, and some of the strange dark-skinned people were striking their tents.

At this point there is quite an accretion of extra-mural buildings, "*foum el bab,*" as they say, "outside the gate." Rows of buildings extend along the sea shore, which now stretches again before me. A little distance eastwards is the corn-market, an open-air enclosure, with nothing very striking about it; and near are blacksmiths and cutlers established in fair-sized shops. I bargained with one Moor for some long curved daggers, and bore them home with me.

The coinage of Tripoli is not encouraging to the simple-minded traveller, who seems bound to lose on all occasions. The *piastre* seems the *pièce de résistance*. One hundred and twenty-eight are given you for a sovereign, one hundred and seventeen equal a Turkish pound, and twenty equal a *mahhboob*. But the Sicilian dollar, the Maria Theresa, and the Austrian florin are a few of the many coins which float in the financial atmosphere, and which one receives as change. If you are swift in your calculations, and wish to make a rapid fortune, by all means set up as a money-changer in Tripoli, and then look out for Englishmen.

A pleasant-looking Moor ambling into the city on his brisk donkey carried a sprig of orange-blossom over his right ear beneath his *sheshya*. He smilingly broke it in two and handed me a piece with which to deck myself.

About six years ago there was an Englishman staying at Tripoli who used to come in from his rides in the Mesheyah bearing boughs of orange-blossom. Oddly enough, he was one of those who held mothers-in-law up to ridicule, and even wrote that when he was inquired of concerning a friend he became very sad, not because the friend was dead, but married. Six years pass away, and I am at Tripoli. "How is * * * ?" asks every one, and I try to look sad in my turn. The orange-blossom recalls a scene in which I took part, and the warning is—be careful in writing of mothers-in-law. They do not forget.

I entered the city by the Bab el Mesheyah, close to the Borj, and almost immediately below the Bab el Fondouk. (The fourth gate of the city opens on to the harbour, the Bab el Bahr, or Sea Gate.)

From the roof of the Locanda, there was an interesting view over the flat roofs of the city. Stepping out through a window, I strolled about, not thinking much of where I was going, and it seems I was walking over some one else's house, the roofs all joining one to another. Looking down into a courtyard I beheld a gay scene, a picturesque group of Tripolitan *houris*, who were playing and singing, a black slave sitting by. It was really a picture—the bright dresses, the jewellery, the handsome faces and dark eyes. Then came a scream, and a seizing of veils and a covering of faces, a rushing hither and thither, exclamations of horror and anger, as they caught sight of the *Roumi* strolling along the roof. I was sorry to have intruded, and returned to the Locanda to luncheon.

In a few moments the black Gharian cook, Muhammed ben Ali, came rushing in in a fright, his white teeth displayed as he rattled away at a tremendous rate. Every one was excited; it might cause a rising against the Europeans; the privacy of *harêm* life had been invaded! Who was it? what had been done? Then I confessed that I was the guilty person, but had erred in sheer ignorance, and that I was very hungry, and would dearly like some *kous-kous-óo*.

CHAPTER X.

IN THE SAHARA.

A cavalcade—The steed of the Prophet—*Al Borâc's* trappings—His voice—Through the Mesheyah—The desert—Its colour—Bedouin and *Bindiggah*—*Hubz*—Ain Zhara—Up a *Nuklah*—*Palmam qui meruit ferat*—Trot to Tripoli—*Al Borâc's* last.

"WE are just off to the desert," I hurriedly added as a postscript to my letter home one afternoon, and then rushed along to Mr. Grace's, where it seemed as if half the donkeys in Tripoli were assembled and showing off their voices.

It would be about three o'clock in the afternoon, when, under the blazing sun, our cavalcade of seven quadrupeds, some equine, some asinine, swept through the Bab el Fondouk, a European caravan on its way to the oasis, Ain Zhara, far away in the Sahara. This was the spot whence Barth set off in March, 1850, on his great travels, and where, in August, 1855, he met Mr. Reade on his joyful return; the oasis where Miss Tinne parted with her friends as she set off to penetrate the land of the Twarigs; and where many a great traveller has rested and gathered together his forces on the first stage of his journey.

A splendid ass, whom, after the winged steed of the Prophet, I named *Al Borâc*, bore my twenty-seven okes, while Mr. Grace, who is a substantial weight, was on a smaller donkey. Between Captain Catelli's long legs promenaded a third specimen of the *Asinus Tripolitanus*, while Signor Morino was mounted upon the back of a fourth energetic and sure-footed quadruped.

The housings and trappings of our brave steeds are simplicity itself. A species of rough sack, stuffed with something softer than hobnails, is rudely fastened on the back of each donkey; a piece of rope is passed loosely over this sack, to either end of which rope is attached a stirrup. It is all delightfully simple; and if by chance a sudden movement causes you to lean any undue weight upon one stirrup, down it goes and up comes the other until your knee is near your chin, a position which is inconvenient as well as undignified when one is at full gallop.

Donkeys and horses take no notice of the bit on this continent excepting as a means of stoppage. You press the reins upon the opposite side of the neck when you wish to turn, but donkeys are sometimes stubborn. Our party consisted of four donquestrians, and three of our friends on Arab horses, viz. the Emir, M. Wittstein, and a German friend from the Locanda.

Since the days of Roman triumphs in the Urbs

Tripolitana surely such a brave display had not astounded the son of the desert.

Away we go, kicking up the dust, accompanied by Jack and Joe, our English dogs, who strike terror into the hearts of the venerable Moors, standing aside for fear of pollution and hydrophobia. Through the bazaars, and between the sentinels at the white city gates, we canter out under the scorching sun. Now through the Mesheyah, with its endless gardens, its olive yards and wells and prickly pear hedges, and its lovely groves of palm-trees, till at last, after about four miles, a halt is called as we approach the verge of the desert, that we may collect our scattered forces, fasten up our girths, arrange our stirrups, etc., and we gather under the delicious shade of a great mulberry-tree near an Arab encampment.

My long-eared friend, *Al Borâc*, is a regular brick. I had my eye on him from the first, and felt perfectly grateful when Mr. Grace suggested that I should take him as my steed. Having found out now how to "wind him up" at intervals, he ambles and gallops deliciously, nearly always leading the whole caravan. He is a pugnacious animal, often trying to get near the other donkeys and deliver a side kick at their shins. I had to discourage him in this practice by the "argumentum ad asinum."

He had a mellifluous voice, which I think would completely drown the most determined efforts of any single camel or donkey in Tripoli. He commenced with a sort of overture, or first movement, in a major key, somewhere below the larynx. This communicated a tremulous motion to the saddle and the rider. Then stretching out his neck and head in one straight line, with his ears well back, he commenced an *adagio* and *forte* movement, going through the whole chromatic scale, and eventually changing to a minor key, until with a sotto voce *finale* he brought to an end the song he loved so well.

Here we are, then, on the edge of the desert. It commences so abruptly that twenty yards one way one is in the midst of the burning sand which extends uninterruptedly to the distant horizon, the veritable Sahara; twenty yards the other way and you are under the shade of the palm, the olive, the caroub, in the midst of the garden of the Mesheyah.

All girths being tightened, in five minutes Jack and Joe, barking wildly, scamper over the rosy yellow sand, followed by our detachment of European cavalry representing England, Ireland, Switzerland, Germany, and Italy, and sending the light dust flying as the strong breezes catch it up from the feet of our energetic steeds and whirl it away in small clouds. I call the colour of the desert rosy yellow; I can think of no more exact indication of its strange tint. Those who saw in the Academy the other year Mr. Goodall's exquisite little picture, "Crossing the Desert," will see how difficult it is to convey by words an idea of the colour of the bright Sahara sand.

A few miles over the undulating desert and the feeling of loneliness begins to come over one. Not a sign of anything but sand. Sand everywhere, blazing yellow sandhills stretching for miles and miles, constantly changing their shape as the breeze whirls the sand along and dashes it into one's face and teeth.

The Emir and I gallop on a mile or so ahead of the others, and his Arab outstripping *Al Borâc* the Winged One, he again passes a couple of miles away, diminishing at last to a black speck on the desert, so that I and the Steed of the Prophet are left alone—just what we longed for.

Alone on the desert, even for a few minutes, what a sensation! I dismounted and walked over the burning sand, leading my faithful donkey by the bridle. Yellow, golden yellow, orange yellow, to rosy yellow, is the vast glaring expanse; here and there the sand gives way to stones, or a hard track is seen where the feet of camels have trodden down the sand. Now and then some little vegetation is seen, but very little—a slight tuft of *halfa*, or a tamarisk bush.

Far away over the waste I see some camels scattered over the desert, trying to find a meal amidst the very scanty vegetation; and beginning to count them I find there are about a hundred and twenty in all. But what is that figure on yonder sandhill, with a long thing sticking out over his shoulder? He is a Bedouin in charge of the camels.

But here is another whom I had not seen before, striding across to me gun in hand. He does not seem to know that I have friends close behind; and fierce enough he looks, his face burnt to a dirty dark brown, his *baracan* over his head, and in his hand the long-barrelled Arab gun, the *bindiggah*.

He intercepts me, and in impolite tones begins an harangue in Arabic, in which he demands "*hubz*" again and again. I told him I did not carry them with me; being quite uncertain whether it was "the antibilious pills" which celebrated travellers always carry in their boots that he wanted, or a pocket edition of Webster's pronouncing dictionary. He became restive and rather impudent in his tone, and suggestively handled his *bindiggah*. For fear *Al Borâc* might become nervous I casually let my white flannel jacket fly back, and his eyes instantly fixed themselves upon a small revolver in my leathern belt.

How the conversation might have terminated I don't quite know, but just then our party appeared in sight, and my friend the Bedouin thought it wise to depart, continuing his grumbling on the "*hubz*" subject. It was bread he was asking for, though that was another way of asking for money. Mr. Grace told him there were plenty of bakers' shops in Tripoli. A Bedouin loses all his romance upon a near approach. He becomes dreadfully practical and very dirty.

Leaving the Sons of the Desert and their camels,

we have a good gallop together, and I could not help breaking into song—

> "From the desert I come to thee,
> On *Al Borâc* shod with fire,
> And the winds are left behind,
> In the speed of my desire."

After about three hours' journey on the heavy sand we approach the oasis of Ain Zhara, where a spring bursts up so freely that it creates a species of marsh, and round it some sort of cultivation is carried on by the Arabs, living in their black goat-hair tents, and here their camels graze on the brushwood growing around. The chief feature, however, is the group of lovely palm trees clustered together close to a mound of fine sand, and towards these palms we urge our steeds.

Out from the black tents flies a whole pack of white Arab curs, at first sight resembling the Esquimaux dogs we are accustomed to see at home. On they rushed, and forward went Jack and Joe, like true English dogs, to conquer or to die. A fierce encounter was imminent, when Mr. Grace slid off his small donkey and lashed the Arab dogs so effectually with his whip that the foe was vanquished.

We rode on to the palms, and Signor Catelli and I ascended the conical hill of red sand on the way. My saddle worked aft and down *Al Borâc's* back, the ascent was so steep. I jumped off in time, and poor Borric and I struggled up through the soft sand, sinking half-way up to the knees, while the saddle descended to his heels. Having replaced it, we reached the summit, and fired a resounding salute, which roused some of the Arabs.

We encamped under the palms, fastening up our seven quadrupeds to the trees. A fearful amount of fun went on in different languages—French, Arabic, Italian, and English, a good deal of the fun centring around our friend the Emir, who understood all. We were beneath the same graceful palm-trees that waved above Miss Tinne and other travellers on the first night of their long journeys, and the desert around us was the same which reaches to the oasis at Djardub, where the rival Mahdi is waiting his time.[*]

[*] I would here venture to quote a sentence or two occurring in a lecture I was invited to give before the Literary and Philosophical Society of Newcastle-upon-Tyne. It is extracted from the report in the local papers. "At Djardub, twenty-two "days south of Ben Ghazi, in Tripoli, is the powerful Zaouia of "Es Senoussi, where, surrounded, we are told, by nearly a "thousand of his followers, and receiving crowds of adoring "pilgrims, the rival Mahdi, Muhammed es Senoussi, lives in "a magnificent building, amidst groves and palm trees. The "people of Tripoli told him (Mr. Boddy), as Mr. Broadley tells "us (in the *Pall Mall Gazette* and '*Tunis, Past and Present*'), "that from the interior caravans of costly presents come to the "great saint, and arms and ammunition are accumulating at "Djardub. A great French traveller describes the Senoussian "Messiah as a 'very fiend for the Christians,' infecting the whole "Sahara with a thorough hatred of the so-called infidel, which "is steadily increasing. Muhammed es Senoussi is forty-one "years of age, and has one arm longer than the other; this "peculiarity especially qualifying him to fulfil a particular

While we were resting I became fired with an unextinguishable ambition to bring down some palm branches which were waving above us. Taking off my boots and socks, I attacked a tall *nuklah* waving over

"prophetic description of the Muhammedan Messiah. Whether
"or no the two Mahdis will coalesce remains to be seen. If
"they do their power will be enormous, for in every town in
"North Africa there are Mokaddem or Vicars of one of the
"two confraternities they represent, and often a large number
"of followers. They hope to drive out the Câfer, the dog of an
"infidel, from Dar-ul-Islam. If the two Mahdis could but be
"persuaded to oppose one another, then Western civilization
"might hope once more to advance in the lands of the
"Crescent."
Since these words were spoken (December, 1883) the Mahdi of the Soudân has made advances to the Mahdi of the Djardub; but Muhammed es Senoussi will have nothing to say to Achmet Muhammed, and no doubt is indignant that the Soudân rising should have taken place and interfered with his own plans.
Herr Nachtigal, whose acquaintance I made at Tunis, has boldly visited the Senoussian Mahdi in his palace at the Siva Oasis. I would quote the remarks of the special correspondent of the *Standard* (October 8, 1884), who has since seen Dr. Nachtigal. Speaking of the Mahdi of the Soudân, he says, "He
"has now addressed a letter to the celebrated Sheikh Senoussi
"in Tripoli, offering him for his moral support the highest
"religious rank in Egypt after the Mahdi has conquered that
"country. In this connection I may mention a remark I heard
"some months ago from Dr. Nachtigal, late German Consul at
"Tunis. Some time before he had been with the Mahdi Sidi
"Senoussi, the celebrated chief of the Senoussi Brotherhood at
"Djardub and the Siva Oasis, whose moral influence extends far
"and wide over that part of Africa. In speaking with Dr.
"Nachtigal of the so-called Mahdi, Sidi Senoussi contemptuously
"remarked, '*What have I to do with this Fakir from Dongola?*
"*Am I not myself a Mahdi if I choose?*' He alluded to the
"title of Mahdi, which is hereditary in his family."

us, and climbed up about seven yards, but it cut my bare feet so much that I had to give in and descend.

I did not like being beaten, and loosing the stirrup leathers from one of the horses, I made them into a circular band to pass behind my back and round the palm in Arab fashion. Then I commenced in real earnest to climb a rougher palm, this time with my boots on, and got on famously until about ten feet from the top, where I hopelessly stuck, as it got smoother and smoother. In my boots I could get no farther; I managed, however, to unlace them and let them drop to the ground, climbing up with my socks on, which I literally cut to pieces before I got down again.

"*Coraggio*," cries Captain Catelli; and after a few desperate efforts, in which I scraped more skin than I could spare from off my arms and breast, at last I succeeded in getting up and breaking off two branches, which I dropped on the sands below. At last I arrived once more on the ground in safety, though very sore and bleeding, and the reader may justly remark that the whole proceeding was a trifle foolish and that I deserved to get scratched.

"*Palmam qui meruit ferat*" seemed too high-flown a motto for me to adopt, so I did not bear my palms home, yet the "winged steed" was decorated with them. They were stuck in his girths, one on each side, and trailed behind, sticking out eight or ten feet as they swept up the sand of the desert on our homeward march. We galloped now by another track towards the great oasis of the Mesheyah, as we crossed the sands of the desert passing some Arabs from the interior patiently trudging along, driving their camels laden with huge burdens of esparto grass.

It was getting dusk as we entered the gardens of the Tripolitan oasis and cantered through the Arab villages, where every one was seated outside, or lying on the road wrapped in the white *baracan*. The *Mueddins* were chanting their long wailing cry, "Allah il Allah! Our Lord Muhammed is the Prophet of God. O come, all ye Faithful, come, come to prayer."

By the roadside are huge pits digged and graven, dangerous indeed to the unwary; they are empty granaries, some twenty and thirty feet deep, and reach sometimes nearly to the middle of the road. *Al Borâc* avoided these carefully, and I trusted him implicitly. I find that in donkey riding, as in other things, it is better to follow custom. The custom is to ride bareback, taking one's seat well aft, so that an evil and ill-disposed ass has no chance of lifting his hind legs to kick. My saddle coming loose on the way home, I rode bareback, discarding the stirrups, and found it comparatively comfortable.

One more song of triumph from *Al Borâc's* powerful lungs as he lifted his nose on high and made an impolite grimace, and then we trotted into Tripoli by the Bab el Mesheyah, sunburnt and sleepy.

CHAPTER XI.

VISIT TO THE PASHA OF TRIPOLI AND TO THE BLACK VILLAGE.

A dish of *svinge*—H.E. Achmet Rassim Pasha—The *nuklah* again—Story of Moslem tree-felling—Marriage and prudence—The Pasha and the murderers—Visit to negro village—Beehives—Black babies—Ethiopian salutation—Regrets and dreams.

Svinge is a very delectable Arab dish. It is made of honey and flour; and, when it comes from the hands of El Hadji Abdullah ben Said el Khartoumi, it gains in attractiveness.

I was discussing such a dish at breakfast one morning on the recommendation of Mr. Grace, at whose hospitable board I was sitting, when the black servant brought a note from the Consulate for me, a Cavasse waiting outside for an answer. Mr. Hay asked me in the letter to go with him that morning to the *Borj* to be received by his Excellency Achmet Rassim Pasha.

Finishing my *svinge*, I repaired to the Locanda, to change from white to black—from a semi-Turkish wanderer in white flannel and red *sheshya* to a black-cylindered, tail-coated, white-collared European. And thus attired I solemnly followed Muhammed the Cavasse as he preceded the *Roumi Imaum* to the British Consulate.

The Turkish Governor-general of the Vilayet of Tripoli, Achmet or Hamed Rassim Pasha, is one of the most liberal-minded of Oriental officials, probably owing in some measure to his having received a Western education. He speaks French perfectly, having been brought up in Paris, and if anything his ideas are a little too Occidental and not sufficiently Oriental to please the Porte.

Achmet Rassim has never held a portfolio at Constantinople, but that he is highly valued by the Sultan is evident from his appointment as Governor-general of Tripoli at a time when alarming rumours were circulating, and when France was advancing her policy of annexation in the neighbouring regency of Tunis.

The Pasha is now an elderly man, and he justly pleaded his age as an excuse when this honour was thrust upon him. His wish had been to end his days in his kiosk on the Bosphorus, where he might have such friends as he chose, without being fettered by the restraints of diplomacy and official etiquette.

Accompanying Mr. Hay and following one of the fine-looking black servants of the Consulate, we proceeded to the castle, here called the *Borj* (in Tunis the *Kasbah*.) A large number of the Moors respectfully saluted our consul as we passed through the narrow streets. At the gate of the *Borj* up went the Martini-Henris as the sentries saluted, and we passed into the quaint, rambling old building.

His Excellency was seated in a pleasant room containing European furniture and a divan in the window recess covered with red cloth. From this window we could see the blue waters of the harbour and the shipping. The Pasha, dressed in European costume, a Turkish fez on his head, came forward to meet us as we entered, and courteously waved us to chairs. Turbaned servants noiselessly handed round coffee in tiny cups of exquisite porcelain, and presented us with cigarettes and sulphurous matches. This is the act of hospitality immediately shown to all callers in an Eastern country.

The Pasha took a pleasant interest in my visit to Tripoli, and carefully inquired as to all I had seen or intended to see. One thing above all else made an impression upon him; that was my climbing the palm tree at Ain Zhara. Again and again he returned to this subject. "But why did you climb the *nuklah*? If it had been necessary, if it had been a duty, then it could be understood, but why endanger life for no purpose?"

It was explained (but without much apparent effect) that Englishmen when young are often trained in athletics, and enjoy the letting off of their superfluous energy in climbing or other active exercises.

As a commentary no doubt upon my proceedings at Ain Zhara, the Pasha told us a story of a young Turk who wished to make himself notorious, and went one day into the woods with an axe, and cut down all the trees he could, in the style of a certain Frankish Vizier. In the evening he returned to the village with his trees on a cart, and a crier going before, crying out, "Behold the trees that Ali Ben Mustapha has cut down; yet not in his own power, but with the aid of Allah."

Later on in our conversation his Excellency inquired if I were married, and when he heard that I was still untrammelled, he replied, "Ah, he would be more prudent if he had a wife!" The Pasha is, I believe, by this rule four times as prudent as any moderately married Englishman.

Achmet Rassim recounted an adventure he had once had when in his younger days he was sent to a savage tribe to arrest some murderers. He went up to the mountains without military escort and unarmed. There he was met by some of the fierce natives, who demanded whither he was going, and tried to stop him by threats. He said he had come to see their chief, and if they touched him they would all be executed, and that he had power of life and death over them all. They were completely cowed, and took him to their sheikh. Achmet

Rassim had the murderers put to death in his sight. The Pasha said he was calm when in great danger, but that afterwards he could not sleep.

His Excellency is apparently about sixty years of age, and wears a short grey beard and a moustache. During our visit he held in his right hand, like a good Mussulman, the rosary of beads used among Muhammedans to count ejaculatory prayers. In his left he held his cigarette when he was speaking. He shook hands with us as we bowed ourselves out of his presence, and pleasantly wished me "*Bon voyage.*"

The Pasha is liberally minded towards the Christian religion, but strongly denounces human mediation between the creature and his Creator. May the Ottoman Government be blessed with many an Achmet Rassim!

The Emir and I visited some of the Pasha's black subjects, who live a mile and a half out of Tripoli, in a native village.

None of my Oriental experiences have left a more pleasant recollection than those at this "kraal," as it would be called in Southern Africa, and my brief friendship with the dark bronze inmates of these beehive huts within the enclosure of the Black Village. Here are gathered dark-skinned people, from chocolate to black—inhabitants of the Soudân, people from Fezzan, Mourzouk, Ghadames, and even from the far-distant West Coast.

One is always struck in Tripoli with the large

proportion of black faces in the streets, and here one sees the origin of it, for these negroes are constantly in the town of Tripoli.

The Emir and I walked out to this encampment, which is on a sandy slope between the palms and the sea shore. Hundreds of *deriba*, as these bamboo and palm-leaf wigwams are called, filled a great enclosure, just as one sees them in pictures of Central Africa. The chocolate inmates were glad to see us, and as they could talk a little Arabic we managed to interchange our thoughts.

Happy, merry people are these fine dark-skinned negroes, ever showing their pearly white teeth—such teeth as no dentist with sumptuous surroundings, splendid instruments, and magnificent fees could ever hope to equal.

Passing within the high palisading of bamboo work, we find on all sides funny little round huts of bamboo and palm, with a hole at one side to creep in by. On entering one we find it very cosy, about ten feet across and six feet high in the centre, where it is supported by a stout bamboo. Insect life, of course, has a luxuriant time of it, and various species of creeping and jumping creatures are abundant. Among the creeping things may be mentioned the gutta-percha babies, which are black from their birthday onwards. Having never handled a black baby before this struck one as remarkable, though of course it is very natural, absurdly natural.

Some of the men are grand fellows. If one obtains one's idea of the negro from the degraded characters found in Northern climes, half civilized, entirely demoralized, and clad in our uncomfortable and unsuitable garments, then one is apt to think badly of the race. But see him at home under an African sun, gracefully clad in some bright red-and-white material, only enough to make him look picturesque, but not sufficient to hide his splendid limbs; see the natural grace with which he does everything, and then you cannot help admiring him.

Here is a young couple sitting beside their bee-hive, the wife with a tiny baby in her lap, and a small india-rubber boy peeping over her shoulder at us, half afraid, half astonished. A piece of money overcomes all bashfulness, and soon he has hold of my hand, while his parents are equally delighted. The mother has her frizzy hair arranged in a fringe of corkscrewy ringlets, which hang round her dark bronze forehead in Fijian fashion; and huge earrings, of about five inches in diameter and made of silver, are partly suspended from her ears, and partly from her black frizzy hair. She has a bright intelligent face, bronze skin, and well-developed broadly spreading nose.

Outside another hut we found several women pounding grain in large wooden basins; one middle-aged dame full of fun as she banged the contents of the bowl before her.

I

We noticed in another part of the village some pleasant-looking women, with deep tattoo-marks upon their foreheads, and found it was the distinguishing sign of the tribe to which they belonged, near the West Coast. We asked what brought them so far from their home, and they replied, "Money." They were daughters of a chief, and had been sold as slaves, and then had escaped and made their way to Tripoli. They had all the ease and self-possession of ladies of position; wonderful dignity, and a becoming simplicity in their manner.

The salutation upon our departure was characteristically Oriental. A chocolate hand was extended, which I expected to shake, but as we offered our hand in return it was only slightly touched, with a profound reverence, by finger-tips. The hand which had touched ours was first pressed to its owner's lips, then the forehead was solemnly touched (the head being inclined), and finally the black hand was laid upon the heart.

These negroes are nearly all Muhammedans, and in the centre of their village is the hut of a black *Marábout*, who goes about with a white beard, a black face, and a green flag—a droll-looking old "Christy minstrel," who has, I am told, perfect command over his coloured troupe.

I left the village with some regrets, and often still I see those round beehive huts, with the little gutta-percha babies crawling in and out of the hole where you expect the bees to appear ; I close my eyes, and the palm trees are waving around that oddest of villages, their graceful branches shivering in the breeze ; I hear the merry laughter as those splendid teeth part so good-naturedly ; the swarthy graceful forms, the bright light dresses, the happy faces baking under that burning sun,

> "Where the women all work for fear the men beat,
> Where there's *legmi* to drink, and *kuss-kuss* to eat,
> And the camels they never cease groaning
> As the sun beats down on the sand."

CHAPTER XII.

A SUNDAY IN TRIPOLI.

Sunday observance—Three sabbaths—English service—Baptisms—Florence Mary and Macdonald Nugent—The upper room—The Eleven—Christianity and Muhammedanism—Father Angelo—Madame Gagliuffi—Sunday thoughts.

To rise on Sunday morning and find everything going on exactly as on all other days seems at first very strange to an Englishman. The swarthy porters bearing their huge burdens along the narrow streets, the cries of the Arabs, the dusky bakers shovelling the loaves out of their deep ovens, the bazaars busy and noisy, the picturesque crowds hurrying hither and thither in the hot sun—all this is very un-Sunday-like, and must in time affect the reverent ideas almost naturally implanted in English minds.

Three Sundays in every week—Friday, the Mussulman; Saturday, the Jewish; and Sunday, the Christian; this must weaken the observance of any one day. The result is, that on Friday one sees the Moors in their best clothes streaming into the mosques, but the bazaars seem to be open as usual. On Saturday there is less business, for the Jews, who hold most of the money, strictly refuse to negotiate. On Sunday less outward observance is to be seen, though the Maltese attend the Roman Catholic church in large numbers, and the few English residents meet at the Consulate in the morning, where the Church service is read.

It was a long time since an English clergyman had been at Tripoli on Sunday, and all seemed to be pleased at the prospect of our having service, especially as two little English babies were to be baptized. The service was to be held at Mr. Grace's house, the Consul-general being temporarily a bachelor. His family were in Europe.

It was a novel feeling to have for an apparitor a splendid black fellow in flowing drapery, while another solemn, turbaned Muhammedan stood at the door of the drawing-room which was to-day to be our church.

In the presence of most of the English inhabitants I baptized " Florence Mary " Grace, and " Macdonald Nugent " Crabtree, the latter the son of the telegraphic manager at Tripoli, the former the pretty blue-eyed daughter of my kind friends the Graces. All the English residents were present at our morning service, which was held afterwards. Madame Gagliuffi at the harmonium accompanied the hymns, and every one helped to make it a hearty service.

The windows of our upper room looked into

the narrow street, and of course were open. Once or twice, as we were singing the glorious old hymns, "Rock of Ages," or "Nearer, my God, to Thee," I thought I heard a shout of derision or disgust from the Arabs in the street below. Possibly this may not really have been the nature of the noise, for the Moors seem to have a strange way of shouting at all times, instead of speaking. Though all the English residents were present, of course our congregation was small. There were but "eleven in the upper room." The number and the place suggested to one's thoughts the meeting in another Oriental city, where eleven were gathered also in an upper room, the doors being shut for fear of the Jews.

Missionary efforts among the Muhammedans are of a most disheartening character, and so far have not been attended with any palpable results. North Africa, from Alexandria to the Straits of Gibraltar, was at one time Christian. The Church in the seventh century was failing as the Donatist schism sapped its strength. Then came waves of fierce Moslem fanaticism, deluging the country with blood, carrying the religion of the camel-driver of Mecca at the edge of the scimitar, until Christianity was driven back into Europe.

At the present there are no native Christians in North Africa save the Coptic Church in Egypt; and no English missionaries along the whole of Algeria, Tunis, and Tripoli. The few Roman Catholic missions I am told make no headway, though they succeed in cultivating friendly relations with the natives by acts of kindness, such as supplying medicine and advice to those who are ill, but they make few converts. When in this wide world there are so many fields far more promising, where the seed brings forth sixty and a hundred fold, does it not sometimes seem like a misdirection of spiritual energy to attempt to sow on hardened soil?

The Muhammedan religion owes all its higher morality to the pure Gospel of Him whom Muhammed certainly recognized, but as a prophet only. Part of its creed is avowed hatred of the infidel, that is, of every one who is not a Muhammedan. Then it is much easier to be a good Muhammedan than a good Christian. With the Moslem outward observance is sufficient to win for him a sensuous heaven. His chief duties are a recitation ofttimes of the creed, "God is God, and Muhammed is his prophet," a journey to Mecca, observance of the five hours of prayer, fasting *during the daytime* in the month Rhamadan (when the Korân came down from heaven), and hatred of idolatry and of Jews and Christians.

This surely is less difficult than the strait gate and narrow way of the pure religion of the Nazarene. It is infinitely harder to be forgiving on all occasions, to love our fellow-men as much as ourselves, to be perfectly honest, perfectly pure, perfectly truthful, to seek not self but the welfare of others, and when all is done humbly to feel that we are unprofitable servants, and must trust in an all-powerful Mediator.

The secret of success in the aggressive propaganda of Islamism lies, I think, in the fact that a mere tacit consent is required of the converts, without any thorough knowledge of the doctrines they embrace. They give up their idols of wood and stone, and must worship the one God of heaven and earth; but they are allowed to keep their wives (that is, four), and others not bearing that name; they are encouraged to fight for the Faith in the name of the Prophet, and so dying they are received by dark-eyed *houris* in Paradise.

With my friend the Emir I went on Sunday afternoon to see the *padre prefetto*, Father Angelo di Sant' Agata. Religious differences are much diminished in the presence of a common adversary and in a distant country, while a conscientious servant of his Master, like Father Angelo, is deserving of all respect, even from those who look at the Truth from a different standpoint. Vespers were just over as we entered the courtyard, out of which the church and other buildings open. The Maltese congregation was passing out, men, women, and children, all most respectably dressed. The church is rather small, and is about to be replaced by a larger building. We went up a flight of steps out of the court to the *padre's* house, and were shown into a pleasant room with framed photographs of familiar Italian towns upon the walls, and tastefully furnished in European fashion.

In a few moments the *padre* entered. He was fairly tall, with a long grey beard, and dressed in the Franciscan habit. Few faces have I ever seen where kindliness, honesty, and determination were more pleasantly stamped. For an hour or so we conversed on many subjects: about England, Manning, Newman, our new Archbishop, and even of Bradlaugh, of the *Sangue Christiani*, of his travelling experiences, and of my own. The father has travelled among the natives of the interior, in Fezzan, and along to Ben Ghazi, and has always received kindness. He has an hospital here in Tripoli, open to all comers; and the stories of his kindness travelling before prepared for him a warm reception from the negroes of the interior.

After a very pleasant interview we left the kind old *padre* and went to the Belgian Consulate. Madame Gagliuffi (once Miss Dickson) had enjoyed our little service in the morning very much, and by her kind expressions made me feel more than repaid for anything I had done or said. M. Gagliuffi was once our vice-consul at Mourzouk, and in his house are many quaint presents from chiefs of different African tribes. Madame Gagliuffi gave me a souvenir —some African music harmonized by her brother.

In the quiet of my room in the Locanda that night, I joined with friends at home in our common worship, returning also hearty thanks for the kindness I received in a strange land. The sunlight that had long died away at Tripoli was shining in at the western windows of churches far away to the North, and familiar words seemed to echo across land and sea.

"We thank Thee that Thy Church unsleeping,
 While earth rolls onward into light,
Through all the world Her watch is keeping,
 And rests not now by day or night.

"As o'er each continent and island
 The dawn leads on another day,
The voice of prayer is never silent,
 Nor dies the strain of praise away."

CHAPTER XIII.

THE LESSER SYRTIS.

The last of Tripoli—Greater and Lesser Syrtis—Acts xxvii. 17—Arab passengers on the *Abd-el-Kadr*—Lotophagitis—Lotos-eaters—Why melancholy—Homt-es-Souk—Bony pyramid—Ghabes—Saharan canal—French army chaplain—Père Hyacinthe—The Salvation Army.

In passing from the Pashalik of Tripoli to the Regency of Tunisia the readiest mode of transit is found in some of the Italian or French coasting steamers.

My journey towards the "Holy City" commences now in real earnest, as, with many regrets, I part from my Tripolitan friends on the deck of the *Abd-el-Kadr*. The engine-room bells ring, the propeller churns the dark blue waves as we steam round the great white ironclad from Constantinople, one of the three Turkish men-of-war which now guard the harbour of Tarabolos Gharb.

We leave the town of Tripoli behind us, the curious ships in the harbour, the minarets and the white houses bathing in the sun, and the palm groves stretching far away to the east. Yonder we see the domed *Marábouts* and the English cemetery standing out against the dark green *nuklah* and the red cliffs.

Slowly we pass round the half-sunken rocks; leaving a white track behind us, we steam through the deep blue water on our northward course, which lies through the gulf known as the Lesser Syrtis.

In Acts xxvii. 17 we read in the original and in the Revised Version that the sailors on St. Paul's ship, during the prevalence of the gale from the E.N.E. which first burst upon them from the high land of Crete, fearing lest they should be cast upon the "Syrtis" (A.V., quicksands):

"φοβούμενοί μὴ εἰς τὴν Σύρτιν ἐκπέσωσι"

lowered the gear and so were driven. This is the Greater Syrtis between Tripoli and Benghazi. We are now sailing in the Lesser Syrtis, which lies more to the north-west.

On board the *Abd-el-Kadr* we have a number of Tunisian Arabs and some Arab Jews, all crouching near the forecastle, having taken deck-passages. An elderly female Mughrebi rushes up to me and kisses my hand enthusiastically. I was somewhat unprepared for this exhibition of maternal affection, and did not perhaps reciprocate it enthusiastically. The *Abd-el-Kadr* is a fine boat of the *Cie. Gen. Transatlantique*, a counterpart of the *Ville de Rome*, and its commandant, Captain Holly, a pleasant Frenchman, whose happy face suggests another initial letter to his name.

At seven next morning, the air very heavy and

close, we lie at anchor off the Insula Lotophagorum, the veritable island of the Lotos-eaters.

> "All round the coast the languid air did swim,
> Breathing like one that hath a weary dream."

This just describes the atmosphere to-day as we lay off Lotophagitis. This island of Djerbah, in Lesser Syrtis, has been celebrated from classic times. It is the Meninx of Pliny,* and hither Ulysses came as he returned from the Trojan war. Of its inhabitants Homer tells us that they are

> "Not prone to ill, not strange to foreign guests,
> They eat, they drink, and nature gives the feast,
> The trees around them all their fruit produce,
> Lotus the name; divine nectarious juice
> (Thence called Lotophagi) which whoso tastes
> Insatiate riots in the sweet repasts,
> Nor other home nor other care intends,
> But quits his house, his country and his friends."
>
> HOM. *Od.* Bk. vi.

Some say that it is the wild jube-jube plant, whose berries are the lotos, and others consider it is the fruit of the caroub tree which grows here so abundantly.

This latter is that lotos-bean which by some who know not better is called "locust," and which may be seen in small shops in our towns and in the hands and mouths of our own street Arabs, who thus become "Lotophagi." Some, who err, assert that it was

---

* M. Guérin, in his "Voyage Archéologique," also assures us that the island is the Brachion of Scylax. The Scylax who was sent on a geographical expedition by Darius Hystaspes sailed, however, from the Indus to the Red Sea.

upon this bean that St. John the Baptist subsisted when he lived on "locusts and wild honey" (Farrar, "Life of Christ," vol. i. p. 110).

I did not know before why the adjective melancholy should be always prefixed by the poet when speaking of Lotos-eaters, but on essaying to consume a lotos-bean in its unripe state, I fully realized it all.

So we lie off the island of Djerba, in the shallows of the Lesser Syrtis, and the modern Lotophagi come off to us in their slow-moving craft. Our whistle booms out in an unromantic way over the Syrtean shallows to quicken their movements.

At Homt-es-Souk, near the white houses yonder on the beach, there formerly * stood a pyramid, built not of stones or bricks as is the usual pyramidic fashion, but of layers of Spanish skulls and bones belonging to soldiers who came here under the Duke de Alva in 1560. It has lately been removed and the bones interred in the cemetery of Tunis.

On board this morning the Arab passengers, having performed their religious ablutions and said their prayers Mecca-wards, lie about the deck with all their baggage around them. Under the title baggage no doubt they would include their wives, of whom only one eye was visible. The old Arab woman who kissed my hand yesterday was most anxious to display her knowledge of the French lan-

* Sir Grenville Temple, "Excursions in the Mediterranean," i. p. 156.

guage, and followed me about the decks politely screaming " Banjo." At last it dawned upon me that she meant " Bon jour." I think she must have been an Islamic saint ; she had the essential qualification— weakness of intellect.

A great barge glides up to us over the calm sea, a whole Jewish family in their picturesque costume sitting in its stern. The patriarch is cross-legged and immobile, the mother holds her children close to her, fearful at the new experience, and a pretty little child climbing over the luggage is all innocent of any danger, and happy in her excitement. They settle down in a corner on the deck, with all their family goods, strange pots, baskets, and bags.

Another boat with French officers in sun helmets and scarlet leather trousers reminds us that we are now near a land " occupied " by France. The boats roll and toss, and the passengers scramble on board amid a fierce Babel of many tongues, in which blacks and Arabs enter into close competition with the Frenchmen on board, as to who shall give vent to the most ear-piercing yells.

> " Now round about our keel with faces pale,
> Dark faces pale against the rosy flame,
> The mild-eyed melancholy Lotos-eaters came."

Some of these Lotos-eaters are fine fellows, dressed in a manner which might excite a shade of envy in the minds of ladies of fashion in our own land, accompanied, however, I am sure, by unlimited admiration.

Long red morocco leather boots, or white stockings and slippers, adorning handsome legs and feet, *djubbas* of ruby or green, an exquisite light *haic* tastefully thrown over all, so graceful, so dignified.

The scene forward is very interesting. The Arab families are encamped on the deck in their Oriental costumes, while diminutive but precocious babies crawl about and look up with intelligent eyes at all that goes on. Aged Moors, much troubled with their trying surroundings; mattresses, carpets, bags, and strange packages (some of which you find are human if you sit down on them); French soldiers in faded uniforms, and Maltese women with gay handkerchiefs on their heads.

At last we glide away from the Insula Lotophagorum and sail for hours under the blazing sun, until we see before us the great white dome of Sidi Bulbeba's *kouba* far away on the low sandhills, where the desert stretches from the Tacapean oasis to join the Sahara.

Ghabes is by no means an attractive spot in summer time, especially when the *giblch* (sirocco-wind) is blowing, as it so often does, not in great blasts, but lazily shading the sun with a dusky pink cloud, and bringing up the fine sand and oppressive furnace-heat from the Sahara.

"Through clouds of dust the crimson sun
 Glares on the earth in lurid ire;
 The parchèd earth with thirsty lips
 Is gasping, ready to expire."*

---

* Poems by Archbishop Trench, p. 295.

Through these sandhills it is proposed to cut a channel, and to let the Mediterranean in on to the huge *shotts* or marsh lakes of the interior, which it is asserted are below sea level, and thus to make a vast inland sea, where the smoky steamer shall replace " the ship of the desert." The Tunisians, and inhabitants of the interior, however, love their date palms, which the salt water would destroy.

Ghabes is destined to play an important part in the future, if the Saharan Canal becomes a fact. We anchored a mile and a half from the little jetty, near the palm trees, beyond which is the French encampment. It is here that the great "cut" will be made, and these shallows will require some considerable dredging ere large vessels can pass in.* Over

* The author here ventures to introduce, in the form of a footnote, some remarks made by him in a lecture at Newcastle soon after the visit of the Comte de Lesseps to that town. He gives the words as reported in the Newcastle papers : " In these days of magnificent engineering schemes, when Franco-Caledonian energy and diplomacy overcome obstacles of all kinds in the making and widening of canals, the subject of an African inland sea seems less visionary each year. Many people, however, have a vague and mistaken notion as to the Sahara. They take up an atlas, perhaps not a very modern one, and seeing a large portion of Africa coloured brown and labelled 'the Sahara,' they at once jump to the conclusion that this will be covered by the proposed Saharan Sea, which would then extend from Ghabes to Timbucktoo. In fact, Timbucktoo has so often been referred to as being on the shores of the proposed inland sea, that it is well to be reminded that it is upon the river Niger, some fifteen hundred miles above its mouth, and therefore situated in a country some thousand feet above the level of the sea. It would be expensive

the long rollers we swung in a native boat towards the shore, and all the dexterity of the Arab boatmen work to pump the Mediterranean up to Timbucktoo. Now, the Sahara is not a level desert plain uninhabited by a living creature. There are mountains and hills to be seen continually. There are oases, some of considerable extent, in which are found towns and villages. There are thousands of inhabitants, some of nomadic race, some living in fixed dwelling-places. What, then, would be the effect of letting in the waters of the Mediterranean upon the Sahara? It would probably create a series of huge lakes bounded by mountains and connected by channels. An immense number of towns and habitations would be destroyed, together with countless groves of *nuklah* or date palm, the chief source of food and wealth to many of the Saharan inhabitants. It would open up in time a new traffic and new freights for north country steamers if the holders of the canal saw fit to make it possible for British steamers to compete. Ghabes would become the Port Said of the new canal, and, as such, a most important station in the Mediterranean. At present Ghabes is not interesting. The sands of the Sahara come down to the very seashore, while upon an oasis to the north, a splendid grove of date palms stands out dark green against the heated red desert. Toiling over the burning sand last June, I examined the spot where the canal is proposed to be cut. The Gibleh or Sirocco wind was blowing, hiding the sun behind a pink cloud of Sahara dust, and Ghabes seemed a very forlorn spot. Some ten miles of sandhills separates the Mediterranean from the first of a chain of shallow *sebkas* or brackish lakes which stretch far into the interior, and here the inland sea would commence. These inland marsh lakes have been by some identified with the ancient Palus Tritonis, the scene of Jason's adventures; but Sir Richard Wood, who has studied the whole question, placed the Palus Tritonis between Jerber and the mainland. I had some difficulty in getting off to the *Abd-el-Kadr*, owing to the heavy swell which was running. If a port is constructed here, an immense amount of dredging will be necessary, for the steamers of the French Compagnie Transatlantique have to anchor a mile or so from the shore."

did not prevent my getting "soused," nor did my stick save me from being half torn in pieces by the brawny Moors who sought the honour of landing me in Tunisia.

At present the chief features of Ghabes are the oasis, with its palms and gardens, and the uninteresting French encampment. Over the sands careered Arab horsemen, and down to the sea shore came some of the French soldiers for the latest news from civilization, and to have a good look at the distant hull of the good *Abd-el-Kadr*, all ready to steam northwards again.

Through the rollers once more we pulled. I innocently roused the ire of the Arab boatmen, who thought I was sketching them, when I was only taking notes. I exercised the better part of valour, when I saw that I should have either to desist or to "leave the boat." The latter would have been inconvenient at this distance from shore.

In the evening I made the acquaintance of

> M. G. J. DURMEYER,
> *Pasteur.*
> Aumonier,
> Armée d'Occupation. Tunis.

He had been to Ghabes, and was now on his way back to Tunis, calling in at the different stations. Chaplains in the French army, both Roman and Protestant, wear a Mosaic-work cross, which is suspended round their neck by a broad ribbon. We had some talk on matters ecclesiastical, and upon two subjects in which I was naturally interested, he gave me his opinion in writing. Here is his opinion of the "Gallican Church."

"Le père Hyacinthe est considéré en France comme un chrétien sérieux par les âmes se réclamant de la Réforme, mais il s'est nui considérablement par son empressement à sortir du célibat, et par son attachement à la succession apostolique, ce qui l'éloigne d'une part de l'Église de Rome et d'autre part des Églises de la Réformation."

As to the Salvation Army, M. Durmeyer considers that however it has succeeded in England, in France it has brought down upon itself the ridicule which there kills.

"*L'Armée du Salut.*

"L'armée du salut aurait pu faire du bien en France si elle n'avait pas eu recours à des moyens ressemblant un peu trop à ceux qui sont employés par les saltimbanques. Le ridicule tue, dit-on en France, et les manœuvres de l'armée du salut sont faites pour tuer l'œuvre entreprise par elle. Voilà la seule raison pour laquelle je lui ai retiré les sympathies que m'inspire son programme.

"A bord de *l'Abd-el-Kader*, en rade de Gabes (Tunisie), le 29 Mai, 1883.

"L'Aumonier Militaire,

"G. J. DURMEYER,

"*Pasteur.*"

CHAPTER XIV.

THE CITY OF CUCUMBERS.

Es Fakouse—"Sfax facts"—Country seats—Cucumbers—Bombardment—Mr. Leadbitter—Olive-crushing—Arab funeral—Bakery — Cisterns — Abattoirs — Bazaars — Mosques—Three old Moors—*El Hammam*—Abdul Moulir's house—*Shaôushes*—Cadi—Sponges—Koran text—Ride among gardens—Mirage.

FIVE hours' steaming through the gulf of Ghabes and round the Sponge Islands of Kerkena brings us in the early morning to the roads of Asfachus, or Sfax, which city takes its name from the quantity of cucumbers (*Fakouse*) grown in the neighbourhood.

In the early morning we lie two or three miles from the white walls of this badly used town, so much damaged in 1881 by the guns of the French fleet. Large sailing barges come alongside, and the excruciating steam winch of the *Abd-el-Kadr* succeeds in rousing the most obdurate and determined slumberers.

The country is low, and, as seen from the ship, somewhat uninteresting, sandy, and yellow, with a few hills far away inland.

To the north side of the city are the celebrated country gardens, where the cucumbers prosper. Every one who can afford has a 'lodge in a garden of cucumbers,' surrounded by high clay embankments, with hedges of cacti on the top. On donkey-back, or on foot, the Moor journeys backwards and forwards from his country seat to his business in the city—or even to beg. Apricots, grapes, pistachio nuts, all flourish here, and very attractive are these oases in the desert-like country.

A *balancelle* comes out to us, dashing over the tossing water, with her large felucca-sail set, and heeling over before the fresh breeze as she flies over the curling waves. With an Arab family, we are soon on our way over the two and a quarter miles of intervening blue water, tossing and splashing. The Arab lady, who appears like a heap of clothes in the bottom of the boat, is in a state of abject terror, not from the great waves, but lest the Infidel in white flannel should see her face.

On shore I found the only Englishman, Mr. Leadbitter, at the esparto stores, half a mile or so from the harbour, beyond the crenellated Moorish walls dazzling white in the fierce sunshine.

Mr. Leadbitter was most courteous, and did his best to make my Sfaxine visit pleasant, interesting, and instructive.

With a pleasant young Italian, Carmelo Montibello, I went to see the environs of Asfachus.

It was at this city of Sfax that the Arab revolt against the Bey and against his new masters began, and in consequence this town underwent a bombardment and pillage at the hands of the French. The Bedouins had for some weeks become more and more restless, and at last the clouds of dust betokening their approach induced the bravest of Europeans to take to the sea. Soon afterwards a desultory fire from the French man-of-war, *Chacal*, commenced, and when the French fleet* arrived, a bombardment of twenty-four hours brought about a surrender.

The Europeans lived on board barges and ships, also on short commons. Mr. Leadbitter told me he was glad to return to his house, which, fortunately, had not been destroyed either by Arabs or French soldiers.

Relics of the revolt may be found in some of the European houses. Mr. Leadbitter, among other things, possesses a sacred drum, used by some *Marábout* in the Aïssaouiah festival, and an illuminated Korán. A leaf which he gave me as a souvenir, bears the following words in Arabic, brightly painted, words which others than Muhammedans may well remember. "*In the name of the Great, the very Kind, the All-*

---

* It consisted of four gunboats and nine (!) ironclads. The bombardment commenced on July 15th, 1881, was kept up that day and with the electric light until the next morning, when a landing was effected and the town taken.

"*Loving Allah, who is the Master of all, and has
none above Him. We proclaim for the sake of all
who trust in Him, that one thing only is absolutely
needful among the many important things, and that
is to use the name of God often in prayer, for to pray
is better than to rest.*"

From the esparto stores over the hot plains with the young Italian to see an oil mill. We pass under a white gateway into the quadrangle, and from thence into one of the dark chambers opening from it. Here in the inner darkness strange turbaned forms move about, and a mysterious *djmil*, with outstretched neck and eyes blindfolded, strides round and round a mill in which the olives are broken and crushed beneath an old Roman column. The broken fruit is then taken to an adjoining chamber, where the darkness is still more gross, and being placed in esparto bags, the oil is squeezed out by a primitive sort of press, draining it off into slimy dark wells.

Out into the dazzling sunlight, where we are attracted by the weird sounds from a procession of Moors, who are carrying on their shoulders something which at first looks like the Ark of old borne by Israelitish priests. It is the funeral of an Arab woman, and we join the procession as they sing verses from the Korân. The corpse is borne on a bier covered with a sort of a roof of carpet work. The husband follows, and "much people of the city was with him," for it is usual for every one to leave his employment and follow a funeral procession. At the grave all the mourners stand with faces Mecca-wards, in two long lines, and offer silent prayer. The Imaum stands in front nearer the corpse. It is then placed upon its right side in the shallow grave, while a circle of mourners at a little distance again sing verses from the Korân.

The first night after the burial, as the body lies with sightless eyes turned Mecca-wards, the two dread inquisitors, Munkir and Nakir, come and rouse it to a sitting position. "Was Allah thy God, Muhammed thy prophet, the Korân thy 'Book of Directions,' and the Kaaba thy Kibleh?" If the answer is satisfactory the deceased is suffered to sleep in peace until the Day of Doom, but if not they set to work to torture and beat the poor sinner about the temples with iron maces. This is a trifle inconsiderate.

We visit a group of Arab houses in the country, a village called Tah Hona, and enter a combination bakery where one of the turbaned bakers is reading the Korân to the others. Here is the grain in sacks, here is the circumambulating donkey grinding it into flour, here the dough ready to be placed on the oven, and here the loaves are brought out all hot.

An immense enclosure, to the N.W. of Sfax, seven or eight acres in extent, surrounded with stone walls, contains some hundred tanks of very great age, but renovated by the French since their occupation.

They are all below ground, with small openings in the concrete above like the mouth of a well. The water at the bottom is muddy, and there is very little of it, but Arabs, who have been let down by their friends above, are filling pitchers. They make these cavern-like depths resound to their strange songs and cries as the pitchers are drawn up and borne to the city. The water in Sfax is very bad. Mr. Leadbitter sends four miles every day to a well in the country, where alone good water can be obtained.

In an encampment of Bedouins near the walls we see wild-looking half-naked children, and dark-skinned women, with many coins round their strange faces. They are busy cooking *kuss-kuss-óo* on the fire in front of their tents, and are unusually friendly.

Near the northern gate into Sfax is the meat market, where poor little goats and fat-tailed sheep are ending their lives at the hands of their Mussulman executioners, who, to do them justice, are fairly merciful. "*Bismillah*" ("In the name of the most merciful God"), and the poor little black goat, so full of life a moment before, looks up with glazing eye on the black beard and swarthy countenance.

Yet man must live and goats must die. Leaving the Arabs dexterously taking the skins off their victims to use as "bottles," we pass into the city proper by one of its two gates.

No Christians or Jews live within the walls.

These splendid white walls with their square turrets at intervals, and their two massive gates, protect and preserve the Moor uncontaminated, though the infidel may come in through the day to bargain with him. What a sad falling off to see very unpresentable representatives of the *grande armée* at either gate. But poor Tunis is now "occupied," and the Armée d'Occupation is making every preparation for a permanent abode in the land.

We wandered through the different bazaars, and watched the blacksmiths and joiners at work, and inspected the different shops. Nearly every shop had a new door or a large patch of new wood near the keyhole. This is to be accounted for by the fact, that upon the entry of the French, the bazaars were all burst open and ransacked, the reason given being that some fanatics had fired upon the French soldiers from some of the houses.

We passed the two mosques Djâma 'l Bou Shouisha and Djâma 'l Kebir. Into the latter with its rows of pillars I nearly walked, seeing another door opposite and just thinking it was a covered courtyard. It was well for me that I did not go in, or I might have been obliterated, for the Sfaxines are as fanatical as ever. Green turbans, the distinguishing sign of a relative of Muhammed, prevail to the same extent that black faces abound at Tripoli. Nearly every other person seems to be a relative of the Prophet, and dignified by the term *Shreef*.

We sat and sipped coffee in a picturesque vaulted bazaar, out of the blazing sun.

Opposite us three genial old Moors were arranged on a divan. "There is a thorough old rascal," said Mr. Leadbitter, pointing to one of the turbaned gentlemen who sat nursing his knee, with a merry twinkle in his eye.

"Ah, what are you saying about me, Sidi?" exclaimed our bearded friend in a moment, in Arabic.

"I was telling this Frankish stranger what a good old man you were, O Pilgrim," my companion replied.

The other old men were intensely amused, and all shook their heads at their friend in a droll significant manner, and said, "But you are not good at all, Ya Hadji Mufta;" and they all three enjoyed the joke immensely.

A noble looking Moor rode into the bazaar on a splendid barb, and cried out that he would sell him for an amount equal to £9. He added, that he would guarantee that the animal should never eat less than a certain quantity of much corn a day.

We were invited to inspect the Turkish baths, and found two stout, jolly-looking old Moors becoming attenuated. A good many visits to the Hammam would be necessary before they could pass through the pillars of Kairwân. A Moslem shampooer was anxious to know that I was not displeased with what I saw in the Hammam. Perhaps he saw that I was interested in some noble cockroaches which were disporting themselves upon the slabs.

The house of one Abdul Moulir, at Sfax, for the richness of its Moorish designs, is a sight well worth seeing. It is now used as the "Bureau d'Administration des Arabes," and is occupied by the French.

The central courtyard is decorated all round most profusely with rich colouring in arabesque style, and some of the rooms take away one's breath with their gorgeous Saracenic colouring. Nothing but the brush of an artist could adequately convey an idea of the brilliancy of the scene.

In the ante-room were assembled a dozen or twenty Arabs, all dressed exactly alike, in a dark blue *burnoose*, with a piece of silver lace sewn upon it.

These are a species of native gendarmes, some of whom have not borne the best of characters in the past. One of these *shaôushs* has made the most of the opportunities his office supplies to acquire all the personal property of his relatives who fled to Tripoli at the time of the rebellion. He is now about to purchase some real property.

We mount the roof, and see below us a sea of white buildings, the city wall enclosing the greater part in its circling embrace.

Yonder is the blue Mediterranean, and to the other side the hot country stretches far away, partly wooded in one direction, where country residences and gardens stretch for miles.

Some of the little Sfaxine girls wear a picturesque dress of two bright colours, joined together down the centre, front and back, like Wallett, "the Queen's jester." The Sfaxines, like the Tunisians, wear flowers in their turbans, placed just above their right ear, a graceful custom and worthy of imitation. How refreshing it would be to see men coming to town with a rose or a tiny bouquet peeping out over the right ear, stuck in between the hat and the hair.

We looked in on the Cadi, as he sat in his fine white turban administering some sort of justice. It was a picturesque scene, and interesting, especially when one was informed that he was one of the chief leaders of the revolt against the Bey and his French friends in 1881.

This court of the Cadi is quite independent of the French authorities, and is neither recognized nor suppressed by them, as they do not wish to excite any prejudices on the part of the Moors.

We also entered the "Palais de Justice," where, however, litigation was having a poor time of it. We passed into a courtyard opposite, where an office was filled with Arab sheikhs come to pay the war-tax levied by the French (in all £250,000 sterling).

The vicinity of the Kerkena islands, round which we have been sailing, causes Sfax to be an emporium for sponges. We saw large numbers hanging in the sun, some a good size, but coarse. The sponge-boats lay off at the anchorage.

Being most anxious to obtain one of the large illuminated texts of the Koran, we traversed the whole city, but without success. It must be ordered beforehand, said every one. At last, by the kindness of our friend, we obtained one, bearing the words, "In the name of the most merciful God. Enter thou into the gates of peace."

After luncheon we had a pleasant ride out into the country, all among the gardens, and all along narrow hot lanes between high red clay banks and hedges of prickly pear.

At last we cantered back to the white walls of Sfax; and later we scudded over the waves to the *Abd-el-Kadr*, receiving a thorough soaking upon the journey, as both wind and waves were high, and we sailed often with the gunwale down to the water's edge. As we raced over the rough sea we saw a perfect mirage. A long line of olive-trees left their native soil and appeared to be growing on the shore of a great lake stretched out below them.*

Thus ended my pleasant visit to the town of Sfax, and as my kind guide left for the shore I felt I had much to thank him for in displaying to the stranger-pilgrim the sights of the City of Cucumbers.

* Trusting to a somewhat youthful amanuensis to copy from my diary, I found these olive trees *grazing* on the far shore, and the sponges spoken of above, *lounging* in the sun. Climatic influence is very powerful upon vegetable life, but the pen is evidently omnipotent.

CHAPTER XV.

MAHHDIA, MONASTIR, AND SUSA.

A Kairwân port—Oil on troubled waters—Cape Afrikia—A Mahdi here—Monastir and the Monastiri—Susa and black-eyed Susans—Sensible straw hats—Sunset off Susa—Musical marines—The man in the hammock.

Off Cape Africa.—We are anchored close to the picturesque old fortress-town of Mahhdia, once the seaport of the city of Kairwân, distant only some forty miles inland. An oily cargo is being floated off to us in trains of casks, towed out thirty at a time by ragged Arabs in their boats. As they come along they leave behind them on the sea a widening track of smooth water caused by the oleaginous and soothing nature of this floating freight.

From the shore there is wafted across the water the cries and sounds of a city—children's voices, cock-crowing, the efforts of a demonstrative donkey, and the angry declamations of a Mahhdian dog.

A long rocky tongue to the north of the city stretches into the blue water, bearing on its point some ancient ruins, and near them camels graze and

Arabs wash themselves. This is none other than Cape Africa (or Afrikia), from whence Hannibal departed when he left the Dark Continent, a disappointed man, flying from his secret enemies in Carthage and his open enemies from Rome.* Along the shore great yellow rocks receive the attacks of the blue rollers, while beyond the city the country seems in great measure to be wooded and fertile.

This town of Mahhdia, or *Mahdi-ya*, owes its name to one of the predecessors of the Mahdis of our own times. A Mahdi is no new invention; there have been several before Muhammed Achmet of the Soudân and the Senoussian Sheikh. The founder of the fortress-town of Mahhdia was known as El Mahdi Califa. He made no little stir in the Dar-ul-Islam, and for a time was Emir of Kairwân. He was the founder of the Fatimite dynasty.†

The water here is so exquisitely clear that, leaning over the rails of the forecastle deck, I can see the huge chain cable stretching away to the very bottom of the sea, and the anchor half embedded in the ground, while the fish sniff and nibble in an inquisitive sort of way, wondering whether or no it is edible.

* Those who dwell at the other extremity of the Dark Continent scarcely realize that perhaps from this cape, but certainly from this land of Tunis, in the ages when it formed the province of *Africa Propria*, the whole Libyan continent gained its present name—Africa.

† See "Good Words," October, 1884,—"Muhammedan Mahdis;" also "Country of Moors," p. 148, for a quotation from Leo Africanus on this point.

L.

At last our whistle booms out, and is promptly answered by a Mahhdian donkey on shore, who bids us farewell in his native Arabic. The propeller churns the water into a mass of white foam, a lovely contrast to the blue sea around. The sun gets higher and higher as we sail along, until at mid-day our shadows are a mere circle round our feet. An hour or two later the minaret and white walls of another Oriental town may be seen as we approach Monastir.

A long sandy shore, fringed by brushwood, stretches from the "port" to the town, which is a mile away from this primitive landing-place, where there are just a few sheds to protect one from the fierce sun. An old fort with seven port-holes protects the anchorage. It is a Moorish building, with a watch-tower rising above its walls.

The white houses of Monastir are scattered over the promontory, and the feathery *nuklah* rises here and there. Camels solemnly pace the sands, and an energetic donkey ambles along, for its owner wishes to catch the steamer, and soon his boatmen pull lustily from the shore. The arrival of a large vessel is an event in the little world of Monastir.

This Monastir is considered to be the Ruspina of Cæsar. In those old days, as now, the Monastiri were not renowned for "ses politesses ou ses delicatesses." If you have no snarling dog to put at your door, place one of the Monastiri there; such is the adage of Barbary. A couple of hours later we are steaming round the promontory and the brown rocky islets, and see the city from its other side as we sail again northwards.

At last, as the afternoon wears away, my voyaging along the Tunisian coast draws to a close, for here we are, opposite the crenellated walls of Susa, whose buildings cluster together on a gentle slope rising from the blue sea to the Kasbah, which stands on the hill-top.

Susa is well worth a visit. During my short stay here I made my home still with Captain Holly and my friends the French officers, rowing backwards and forwards to see the town and to make arrangements for my journey of one hundred and fifty miles among the Bedouins.

A black-eyed Susan in his gaudy clothes accompanied me round Susa. We went through the picturesque bazaars, and I sat cross-legged upon the shelf in front of an arabesque store, bargaining for brilliant leather slippers.

Some of the buildings of Susa are decidedly handsome. The gates in the city walls are most picturesque—deep Moorish archways with covered ways leading to a second gate inside. We ascended the narrow streets up the hillside on which the town is built, and watched the Arabs plying their different trades. From the top of the narrow street, with its irregular buildings, we looked down over the city and out to the blue sea beyond.

Passing through the Kairwân gate into the country we saw a huge hat coming along, with six legs beneath. It was one of the tremendous straw coverings which the natives wear, useful both as hat and parasol; indeed, it preserved the donkey's complexion, as well as that of the Moor upon its back, whose brown legs almost touched the ground. We wandered through the Jews' quarter, and peeped into strange interiors in passing, startling the families within. They were horrified by my appearance at their doors. "He is an accursed Turk," remarked a large-eyed Jew boy.

Julius Cæsar was really ubiquitous. He has been here in Susa, though they called it Adrumetum then. He landed three thousand foot and one hundred and fifty horse, and trotted round these white walls himself.* I wonder if he found it as broiling as it is to-day. There are two mosques in Susa—El Djâma 'l Natreddin at the south, and El Djâma 'l Kebir, near the Bab-el-Bahhr, neither very interesting.

At last, after walking immense distances in the hot sun, we pass out on to the shore by the Bab-el-Bahhr and make for our boat. As we walk down we meet some Arabs bearing on a pole between them a magnificent turtle which had just been caught. I

---

* Susa was the scene of many stirring events in the past. In the sixteenth century, when it was given up to piracy, the great Andrea Doria reduced the city to subjection; but it soon after welcomed Dragut within its walls. In earlier times Okhbah, the builder of Kairwân, resided here for a long period.

wondered if it was my friend from Gibraltar. Propelled by Arab boatmen, we first amble and then gallop over the heavy rollers to the *Abd-el-Kadr* in time for dinner.

We lie at anchor a mile east of the picturesque town, with its machicolated battlements, its Moorish gateways and minarets, and its white flat-roofed houses one above another, surmounted by the great Kasbah.

The sun goes down, setting, perhaps, behind the holy city of Kairwân, and the dying sunlight paints with a rosy hue the sky, the houses, and the water. To the north the quaint mountains of the Dakkul, which I last saw from the deck of the *Glenochil*, stand out purple in the distance and the peak of Zaghowân to the north-east. Beyond the city walls to the south stretch miles and miles of wooded plain, dotted here and there with flat-roofed country houses.

The sunset tints do not remain, as in our northern climate. The moment the sun descends all the brilliant colours disappear. The rosy cloudlets become dark grey, the sea slaty green, and one can scarcely believe that it is the same picturesque scene one beheld but a moment before.

The French sailors are often *drôles*. They must be merry, must drive away anything suggesting *ennui;* they indulge in discordant noises which they call music in the "dog-watches," concertina, two pairs of bones, and a curious instrument like a little drum with a rod sticking out, which they rub with a resined cloth and which produces a sound between that of a drum and a trumpet. "*Voila le regiment*," cries a captain of chasseurs, putting his head into the saloon. Here they come, marching in step round the ship. In front, to show the way in the dark, a sailor tramps solemnly with a lantern. Nearer and nearer they come, breathing out martial strains, and producing a grand sensation and much applause and laughter from the military officers.

Slinging my hammock on deck, I enjoyed the fresh air, despite the scrambling of the ship's cat over the awning, and awoke very early in the morning to see the grey dawn creep over the sea, and the white buildings of Susa glow in the rosy light of the rising sun, as it rushed up from the eastern sea fiery and red.

CHAPTER XVI.

ACROSS THE SAHEL TO KAIRWÂN.

A farewell dinner—Off to Kairwân—Obstructionists—Last view of Mediterranean—Es Sahel—Francesco Bonichi—Moureddin—Berbers—Waggons—Sheep and goats—Steppes and Sahel—Kairwân and El Kûds—Tramways—First view of the Holy City—Camel dentistry—Well near Kairwân—Snails—Tamarisks—Cicalas—Gloomy Kairwân—Camel dissection—Locanda—View from lattice—Kairwani concert.

A MERRY party assembled in the splendid saloon of the *Abd-el-Kadr* to dine together for the last time before my departure for Kairwân. As it was a farewell dinner the commandant in my honour ordered up sparkling champagne, in which the officers pleasantly pledged my health and "Bon voyage à Kairwân." I proposed in return, in a purer and less expensive liquid, "À la France, et à sa prosperité."

".Ah," remarked a colonel of the Chasseurs d'Afrique, "notre ami Anglais n'joute pas *en Tunisie.*" They all seemed to be convinced that my mission was in some way "diplomatique."

"Parbleu," remarked a Frenchman at the Grand

Hôtel at Tunis, "vous faites un voyage solitaire jusqu'à Kairwân dans le mois de juin, et vous nous dites que c'est pour votre plaisir! c'est incroyable et difficile à avaler."

The sun was high in the heavens when over the blue waves my Arabs pulled away for the last time from the dark sides of the *Abd-el-Kadr*. I re-entered Susa through the great Bab-el-Bahhr, followed by the bronze Arab boatmen bearing my various packages. Passing along the winding streets, with their picturesque Moorish crowds, we were soon at the vice-consulate, where my *carosse*, with a little Maltese *cuccier*, was to wait for me.

My effects having been stowed away in the interior, and my revolver with its little cartridges safely tucked in my belt, the word of command is given, adieus are waved to the little gathering at the Consulate, and I am really off on my solitary journey—the last stage in the pilgrimage to the "Holy City," and far the most exciting. My four little horses, all abreast, dash along the rough street, suddenly, however, to stop, as the way is blocked by a dozen oily camels, wandering all over the road, and bearing black hairy goatskins, which are distended in a dropsical manner with olive oil. "Oh, thou goat-beard! oh, Abdullah, thou fatted ass, why dost thou not attend to thy cattle?"

The unfortunate camels are anathematized in Arabic and Maltese, and with all their ancestry consigned to Jehennum. What was more effectual and practical, they are also promptly battered out of the way. We rattle out through the sea gate, passing away from the crowd of dark-faced Moors, who mutter "*Câfr*," "*Käyrawân*," "*Ma maleh.*"

Susa is built upon a steep hillside rising from the sea. We might have driven up the main street, which ascends the hill to the Kairwân gate. The "oolitic upheaval," however, which in that narrow passage painfully attracts one's attention to the occasional presence of paving stones, would have endangered both *carosse* and its infidel contents. So passing out at the lower gate, we encircle the walls, climbing the hill outside, and arriving at last opposite the Kairwân entrance.

From the hill-top is a lovely view, as one looks back and down upon the blue Mediterranean, with the little vessels far away below, while on its bosom we see the two sloping masts and dark funnel of the *Abd-el-Kadr*. Leaving now the white crenellated walls of Susa behind us, and its Kasbah, above which floats the blood-red flag (for it is the Muhammedan Sabbath) we set out on our long journey, bumping and rattling under the pitiless sun, the earth and sky each like an oven.

We are travelling over the "Sahel," that vast plain which stretches along the Tunisian littoral, and inland as far as the distant mountains, which are faintly discernible to the north-west, round about Zaghowân.

Over a camel track, sometimes scarcely visible, sometimes spreading out an immense width, along this my plucky steeds drag the *carosse*, now bumping over a channel made for irrigation, now crashing through patches of underwood, and travelling the while over a sandy desert-like waste, where for miles no living creature may be seen, and upon which the sun expends its concentrated vehemence.

My Maltese driver, Francesco Bonichi (whom I find it convenient to call Chicco), was not an intensely interesting character. Self-sufficient he was, ready to bully but easily cowed, and yet withal, I think, he was honest. My four brave steeds were accustomed to the blaze of an African sun, or the howls of rage and disgust with which he startled these unfortunates would simply have scorched and blistered their brown backs.

Chicco talked Maltese, which is almost an Arab dialect, so of course could understand Arabic and make himself understood. Strangely enough, Arabic was our chief medium of intercommunication, for he was innocent entirely of Italian, French, or English, and so as an interpreter Chicco was not a great success. When I say that Arabic was our chief means of communication, I do not necessarily mean to imply that our conversation was uninterrupted and everflowing.

Some miles after leaving Susa, we skirt extensive olive yards, with their gnarled trees and greyish foliage. We emerge at length upon a bare rocky plain, sprinkled thinly, however, with stunted brushwood, in the distance resembling English moorland dappled with brown heather, and over this the little horses tug and strain, keeping up a very fair speed.

A small caravan at last meets us—innumerable camels and asses, driven by bronzed Arabs, some wearing the monstrous straw hats of the Djerid, a yard across. They all dart unmistakable glances of hatred at my Maltese, with his four horses. We are jerked, bumped, and rattled along the lonely camel track, until about an hour and a half from Susa we see the white houses of Moureddin, the only village we pass on the way to the Holy City. We enter its narrow street, where the male inhabitants, in their *baracans* and *djubbas*, crouch in the shade, and watch us with no friendly gaze.

With a rush, our brown steeds take us out again on to the hot plains, through huge hedges of *hendi* or prickly pear. We pass a white stone well just outside Moureddin, where the brown women are drawing the water, and discussing topics generally brought forward in our country at " afternoon tea."

They are not at all bashful, as no male relative is in sight, and they make no scruples as to displaying pretty brown faces fringed with hanging silver coins. Very picturesque are these Moors, balancing their earthenware pitchers, or drawing them up from the dark glistening well.

Some miles further on we meet a small company of Berbers with their donkeys and camels, their dogs and children. The latter seem afraid of the Evil Eye,* and run to their parents, while the women discreetly veil their faces, their lords and masters being near. The white dogs make a rush at the *carosse*, but wooden wheels are not pleasant things to fix the teeth upon, and they wisely desist.

The Arabs use a rough two-wheeled cart to bring down the *halfa* grass to the sea coast from the interior. I expect they are something like the waggons of Egypt, which Joseph sent by the flat coast to Palestine to bring Jacob and his household to Goshen. We meet a train of half a dozen of the carts, laden with esparto, drawn by sturdy mules, and driven by swarthy young Moors.

As the afternoon wears away, and we drag heavily over the lonely far-stretching plains, we approach some enormous flocks of fat-tailed sheep and black hairy goats, all grazing as best they can upon the scant herbage. The sheep are burdened by the huge lappet of wool and fat which hangs as a caudal appendage, knocking against their heels, while very long ears are pendant on each side of their sad faces.

The black goats, with perky tails exalted skywards, and mischievous little black horns, caper about

---

* To guard against the effects of the Evil Eye, a charm is seen everywhere in the form of a human hand cast in metal.

bleating in an inquiring manner, near their Arab shepherd.

The plains grow sandy and desert-like, everything burnt up beneath this fiercely scorching sun, though in winter time this wilderness blossoms like the rose after the torrential rains. For hours we do not see a living creature, but towards the end of the afternoon we meet a caravan of diminutive donkeys, all carrying bolster-like sacks of wool, hanging almost to the ground on either side in pannier fashion.

Their owners, stick in hand, march quickly behind them, in their brown *djubbas*, with the hoods over their heads because of the sun. They scowl unpleasantly and pass on. To the north and west, we may see through the heated air the faint outlines of the Zaghowân mountains, and between us and them a huge *Shott* or freshwater lake, the Sebka Kelibia, whose distant waters glisten beneath the sun. On our left, to the south, some miles away, is another immense *Shott*, its great sheet of fresh water lying all calm in the heat, and stretching for an immense distance. It is known as the Kairwân Lake, or as the Sebka Sidi el Hani.

This interminable plain has very much of the character of the Russian steppes in the land of the Cossacks of the Don. It need only the rude *telega*, drawn by patient oxen, and driven by the uncouth Moujik; or the Cossack galloping by on his wiry steed, to take one to the littoral of the Azov.

The distance from Susa to the Holy City is very much the same as that from another Mediterranean seaport to another Holy City, "El Kûds," holy alike to Muhammedan, Jew, and Christian. From Jaffa to Jerusalem is a road now well known to Europeans, and in these days of "personally conducted" tours to Palestine, and Hotels in the City of David, that journey has doubtless lost some of its romance.

The plain over which we are travelling was crossed by one division of the French army in 1881, when advancing on Kairwân, and they then laid a line of tram-rails as they went. These still lie there under the African sun, now disappearing among the tamarisk bushes and now lying on the camel track.

When one is on a solitary journey among the Moors it is humiliating to come across a tram line in the middle of the Sahel. Yet any tendency to fancy that one is in no danger from the Bedouins is soon put an end to on meeting a caravan of these scowling Orientals, who would not be deterred, if they had made up their minds to mischief, by the presence of tram-rails.

At about five in the evening (June 1st) we are approaching an eminence from which we shall obtain the first view of distant Kairwân, nearly twenty miles away across the plains.

The *Marábout* of Sidi el Hani, with its white *Koubas*, is before us above the dark fig trees upon yonder hillside. For a moment we stop and sip a cup of coffee, and then our Barbary horses are set to it once more as we heave and toss, travelling over the plains of the Sahel, on a south-westerly course.

5.40 p.m. *At last.* I make Chicco stop as I alight, and gazing intently over the great plain below us, which stretches to the foot of the distant Ousselat mountains, I see in the far, far distance the white buildings of the city of Okhbah and the *Minar* of the Djáma 'l Kebir.

As I stood on that slope beyond Sidi el Hani, the sun declining to the western hills beyond the Sanctuary of the Moors, I felt a sensation not often experienced, as I looked down upon the city of the "Great One," Okhbah, Kairwân the Holy. It was such a view as this that Dr. Tristram had in 1857, when he felt it not wise to attempt an entry because of Moslem fanaticism. But I knew of the existence of a French camp not far from those white walls, and though I had no friends there, I felt that I should have a means of escape if any serious trouble befell me. The Moors are full of deadly hatred of the European, I could not expect any help from them; the French viewed my presence in the country with some suspicion; but, as the sequel will show, I was indeed fortunate, entering as I did the holiest mosques in Africa, and leaving the city without having ever to seek protection.

We had yet some hours' journey before us, and

could scarcely hope to arrive before dark, though Chicco's team pulled well as we rolled along over the great Sahel-plain.

We cross a *wady*—the bed of a river, now only a muddy gully, and over it a narrow, shaky, wooden bridge, without railing or parapet. Four horses abreast cannot get over, so one is unhitched, and I lead him over after the *carosse*. It was here that M. Jacassey sketched the Bedouin boy on the bullock the year before.

The sandy desert plain is dotted most regularly with tufts of coarse *halfa*, so that in the distance it even looks like prairie-land, though as we rattle along the breeze lifts the sand in blinding hot clouds, penetrating everything. I see near the track the bleached skeleton of a dead camel, and I give Chicco the necessary poke in the ribs, my prearranged Arabic signal for a halt. Taking up the white skull, blanched by the fierce sun, I dash it again and again on some stones until I have loosened its teeth. These huge grinders have been carefully preserved, as visible evidence of the nature of a camel's bite.

6.45 p.m. The purple mountains look very majestic as the sun descends and the sky assumes its lovely sunset hues. Nearer and nearer we approach the Holy City, and we meet some Arabs setting out for a night journey. They do not look pleasant, but one and all exhibit gleaming white teeth.

The sun is just touching the hills as we approach

ON THE SAHEL. SIDI EL HANI IN THE DISTANCE.

a *beer*, or well, on the sandy plain, where a cluster of wearied donkeys and camels are enjoying themselves beyond measure as their drivers let down their pitchers and earthenware *baradas* into the water and draw for them. The whole scene is a brilliant Bible picture, taking one back to the days of the patriarchs. I stand a few paces from the well and take notes as Chicco waters the exhausted horses, each one terribly eager for the first drink.

The sun, which has been burning and scorching all day long, now for a moment rests upon the dark hills, and tints everything with a rosy colour, painting alike the white stonework of the well, the laden camels, the donkeys (all but hidden beneath their esparto burdens), and the wild-looking Arabs in their *djubbas* and *burnooses*. They are looking daggers at Chicco, who unconcernedly defiles the water by letting his infidel bucket down. The water smells atrociously, and yet the Arabs drink deeply of it. A long stone trough stretches from the well, for watering the camels. Everything is bathed in a deep rose colour, for gold, and scarlet, and vermilion is the sunset over the Ousselat mountains, and Kairwân stands yonder, grey and dim before us.

Another hour will now bring us to our journey's end. As we heavily drag over the last few miles on this weary plain, I am attracted by a strange white substance upon all the brushwood around. On stopping to examine the plants, I find the white desert snail in such abundance upon every twig of the tamarisks, that at first sight it seems as if the bushes are covered with blossom or fruit, while the ground below is strewn with the shells of dead snails. I break off some twigs to bring home, and on one piece four inches long count fifteen snails, so that scarcely anything else is to be seen.

Dr. Tristram identifies them as specimens of the *Helix candidissima* and *Helix variabilis*. We compared them together on my return with his specimens brought from Kef, and find perfect correspondence between them.

From the bushes all around bursts forth a shrill noise like the escape of steam from a high-pressure engine. The sound is heard loudly above the rattle of the wheels. It is as astounding a sound as that of the frogs in a marsh. This noise, which we hear in the semi-darkness, is produced by the *cicala*. The other day in Malta a lady said, "I must apologize for calling when you are just going to dinner, for I can hear that you are frying your fish." It was however, only the *cicalas* in the garden.

7.45 p.m. Gloomy and weird are the walls of the Holy City, as at last we approach them in the semi-darkness. We can just see the great *Minar* standing up against the sky above the dark houses, and we pass strange forms moving stealthily over the mounds beneath the great walls.

To-night we must remain without the walls, as

the gates will be now closed. A somewhat disreputable *Locanda* in one of the extra-mural suburbs, kept by a Maltese or Frenchman, is, it seems, the only place, save under the open sky, where one can sleep. It is a drinking-place for the soldiers. At Kairwân, however, one is prepared to put up with anything. Hither then I direct Chicco, who with a dreadful yell of profanities endeavours to prevent the poor horses from falling exhausted to the ground. They struggle on bravely, having travelled quickly since the morning (not much less than forty miles) without rest, and without any refreshment save water. They will soon have a long rest now.

We drive on and on until the *carosse* stops with a jerk, and our equine quartette will not move an inch. It is a dead camel that is in the way, and the road here is narrow. In the darkness the *djmil* has a strange look, for its head and neck are lying a little distance from its body, and its Arab owner is busy taking its skin off its ribs to sell in the Souk el Djulludin.

Under the shadow of the great walls, on and on, until at last we arrive at a *Locanda*, full of drinking soldiers. They give way to no outburst of hospitable delight upon our arrival, but I bring in my luggage, and express my determination to stay. So I am shown at last a bare white room, wherein is a pallet, upon which I may sleep if I am insect-proof.

Here I am then, under the very walls of Kairwân the Holy, for their crenellated summits rise in front of my open casement, and I could easily throw the soap I take out of my portmanteau into the midst of the city of Okhbah.

Leaning out of my lattice, I look down on a truly Oriental scene. Just below me, lit up in the dark hot night by the lanterns hung upon the walls, is an Arab *café*. Here sallow Kairwânis sit on esparto mats in the open air, vociferating and smoking. Wild and picturesque they are in their strange garments, lit up by the lamp, which also illuminates the front of the white Moorish houses, and the great city wall opposite.

Such a Babel of angry, excited sounds comes up to me. They are engaged in some game of chance, four playing and about sixteen looking on, the onlookers as painfully excited as the players.

Hearing some weird Arab music near, in which a single voice leads, and a chorus joins in occasionally, I summon up courage to search for its origin. Putting my revolver in my belt, I grope my way along in the dark, until turning a corner I come upon a scene which was truly a living picture out of the "Arabian Nights' Entertainment." At an outdoor *café* beneath the great walls is being held an Oriental concert. A crowd of Kairwânis, in their turbans and gay costumes, are gathered near a few lamps fastened to the city wall. The Moors all recline on esparto mats placed upon the ground, near two central figures who play a *bindir* (tambourine) and a sort of guitar called a *gimbrih*. The effect is very weird as the whole crowd joins in the quaint chorus. Arabs have strong lungs if they have not a strict ear for harmony. The music is something between a Gregorian chant and a Salvation Army chorus, only always slightly out of tune.

A Moorish attendant was moving among the Kairwânis, and I made bold to recline upon a vacant mat, and to ask for *garhoor* (coffee). When I saw the Moor's expression, I wished I hadn't, especially as the attention of my Kairwâni neighbours was unpleasantly attracted to my semi-Turkish dress. I paid for my cup of coffee, and felt easier when I had moved into the darkness again, and heard the weird chorus from a distance.

My Maltese, Chicco, having extracted some money from me, has disappeared. He knows that he is to be ready to start again in four days for Tunis; but where he has gone I know not.

Returning to my room, I push everything against the lockless, boltless door, lie at last on my pallet, very tired, and am soon in dreamland. Yes, I am back in the Middle Ages now? Verily it is the year of the Hedjra 1300, and I lie beneath the shadow of the walls of Kairwân! Oh Shade of Okhbah the Mighty, and Spirit of Lord Muhammed's Companion, be hospitable to a Wanderer from the Isles of the North! My dreams, however, were destined to be somewhat brief.

CHAPTER XVII.

THE HOLIEST SPOT IN AFRICA.

A cry in the night—Mueddin-roar—Inconsiderate Arabs—Enter the Holy City—The Great Mosque—Quadrangle—Roman inscription—The *Minar*—*Adzân* in English—View over Kairwân—The "Don't-know" mountains—The Holy of Holies—Pillar curse and pillar test—The *Mihrâb*—The *Membar*—Roman spoils—Okhbah's dream.

THE experiences of my first night at the Sacred City were unpleasantly mediæval. I had done my best to barricade the door, and had fallen off to sleep, when a horrid roar made me jump up with an almost electric bound.

Opposite my lattice was the great wall of Kairwân, not fifteen yards away certainly. Just above this was the roof of some minor mosque or the tomb of a saint. Well, it might be two or three in the morning, when from this roof came a shout such as only a fanatical Moslem can give. At first one is inclined to put down the tone of such a cry to rage or to despair. Long drawn out, and bellowed with all the force of Arab lungs, the cry seemed to be aimed straight at me—"*Es sallè kheir min en nûm.*" The "no-o-o-o-o-m" was drawn out, and hung on to with all the breath that the Mueddin had, and then followed for a moment absolute stillness in the dark hot night. Far away over the city, however, came an answering cry, faint with the distance, "*Eshehedu enne Muhammed rasūl Allah.*" And then came in a roar from the Mueddin opposite the whole of the *Adzân*, in which the other Mueddins of Kairwân joined.

At last this was over, and I was half asleep, when I was roused by a hideous row below the window, several Arabs calling with all their might for me to come down and admit them. I looked out and in the darkness could see some white objects below me doing their best to get in, but I very much preferred that they should stay outside.

As soon as dawn approached I began to make out the objects in front of my window. The great wall gradually became visible, and I saw that it was built of little light-brown bricks surmounted by crenellations. A little to my right was the Bab el Djulludin or Skinners' Gate, a Moorish entrance which I roughly sketched as soon as it was light. This appears in an improved form upon the cover.

I was fortunate before I had been long at Kairwân in finding a Moor whose fanaticism could be overcome by silver coins, whose politeness made him profess that he understood my Arabic, and who knew the meaning of at least a dozen French words. I never grew fond of Muhammed, I always distrusted him, and yet I found him most useful to me. I applied to the Ferik, the Tunisian authority, for a firman to visit the mosques. The Ferik is supported now by French arms, though he has native *shaôushes*.

Having obtained my firman, I had before me the double excitement of entering Kairwân and then of penetrating the Djâma 'l Kebir. The latter has been the privilege of very few non-Moslems; the former is no longer what it was, for in *sheshya* and white flannel costume I passed between the sentries under the Saracenic gateway with its double arch, and entered the Holy City without opposition. Some people spat as they passed me, and that was impolite. A small boy cried "Dog," "*Kelb*," after me, but when I rewarded him with a copper coin he followed me with smiling face until he obtained another.

We traverse the quiet city by narrow back streets, scarcely seeing any one as we pass along. Women scarcely ever move about in Kairwân; "it is so very sacred." That is the reason given, but it is a little uncomplimentary. The Kairwân ladies when they appear out of doors are invariably hidden in black *haics*, which completely envelop them, and their faces are covered with black veils. It is the women of Kairwân who make most of the brilliant carpets which are so much valued, and one of which lies now in a northern vicarage.

At last we emerge from the narrow streets

MUHAMMED.

to find ourselves before a long low line of white buildings, above which towers the great square *Minar* of the Djâma 'l Kebir. This is none other than the mosque of Sidi Okhbah. Great Moorish doorways with melon-shaped fluted domes above their porches; these open into the prayer chambers or into the great quadrangle where the *Minar* stands. Through one of these we boldly pass, no one seeing us, and find ourselves in the cloisters surrounding the vast quadrangle. An immense quadrilateral space paved with flat stones is baking in the fierce glare, and through the interstices coarse grass forces itself, and flowering plants, some of which I bring away with me.

Underneath this great court are enormous cisterns where the water is kept cool in the cavernous depths below. The keys of the prayer-chamber are not to be found, so we must return this afternoon to enter the holy of holies in this "holiest place in Africa." Yet we will ascend the lofty *Minar* now and look down upon the city of Okhbah. There are one hundred and twenty-nine steps, many of them marble, carved and floriated, evidently the spoil of some Roman temple.

As I was entering the door at the bottom of the *Minar* my eyes were attracted to two large stone slabs made use of in building or repairing. They contain Roman inscriptions, which, however, were so little understanded of the Moors that one is placed upside down. Perhaps, with the many other Roman remains to be seen everywhere in Kairwân, they come from the ancient city of Sabra.* Causing considerable uneasiness on the part of Moorish attendants, I hastily copied the lower one into my note-book.† It runs thus—

    ANTONINI FILII
    AURELIIANTONINI
    DIVINERVAEADNEPOTIS
    TETDEDICAVERUNT

The upper stone, according to Davis,‡ Pellisier,§ and Ximenez,‖ reads:

    HIC MAXIMI I
    RATORIS CÆSAR
    DIVI TRAIANI
    CAED MFECERU

In the *Corpus Inscriptiorum Latinarum* (vol. viii. No. 80) the editor has built up his conception of the

---

* "It was at first Sabra (twelve miles to the north), the ancient Colonia Sabrata, fortified by Justinian, from whence were taken most of the materials of the Grand Mosque; then the Vecus Augusti (ten miles east), situated near the *Marâbout* of Sidi-el-Nane."—Jacassey.

† Mr. Broadley also gives these inscriptions (without comment). I have not just now a copy of his work before me, but my impression is that he makes the inscription run in five lines and not in four.

‡ Davis, Ruin. Cit. in Afr., p. 375, n. 48, 49.

§ Pellisier, Rev. Arch., 1847, p. 263 descr. p. 410.

‖ Ximenez, diar. 1 f. 139, v. f. 240 v.

whole original inscription, of which the above can only have been fragments.

"Pro salute Imp. Cæs. L. Septimii Severi Pii Pertinacis Aug. Arab. Adiab. PartHICi MAXIMI divI M. ANTONINI FILII divi Commodi fratris divi Pii nep. divi Hadriani pron. divi Trajani Parthici adn. divi Nervæ adn. et ImpeRATORIS CAESAR is M. AVRELII ANTONINI pii felicis Augusti Imp. Caes. L. Septimi Severi Pertinacis Aug. f. divi Antonini nep. divi Pii pron. divi Hadriani adn. DIVI TRAIANI Parthici et DIVI NERVAE ADNEPOTIS . . . hanC AEDEM FECERVNT ET DEDICAVERUNT.

"The Roman capitals represent the existing characters. The inscription first of all contains the names and titles of Septimius Severus and his son Marcus Aurelius Antoninus (Caracalla), and their relationship with preceding Emperors. No doubt Geta was included in the original, but his name was struck out when he was murdered by his brother Caracalla."

So writes Dr. Collinwood Bruce, who with his usual courtesy readily interested himself in this inscription. His opinion cannot be valued too highly.

Arabicus, Adiabenicus, and Parthicus were of course honorary titles of Severus and others. These stones were two out of perhaps eight running along the *façade* of the *Aedes* whose erection and dedication it commemorated.

Climbing the *Minar* with my guardian Muhammed,

I found near the top in a corner a dark crimson flag which an irresistible impulse caused me to take up and wave. This is none other than the blood-red banner with which the Mueddin-in-chief signals to all the lesser Mueddins of the other mosques that the moment has arrived for calling the Faithful to prayer. With what horror would the holy Mussulmans of Kairwân be filled if they knew that an infidel *Imaum* had taken the sacred banner into his hands, that blood-red flag with which every Kairwâni is so familiar. How often while at Kairwân did I see that flag waved from the Djáma 'l Kebir and hear the long wailing cry, the *Adzân* or call to prayer,

"*God is All-Powerful.*

"*We proclaim that God is One only.*

"*We proclaim that Muhammed is God's Prophet.*

"*Hark! for Prayer.*

"*Hark! for Salvation.*

"*God is All-Powerful.*

"*There is but One God.*"

To which is added in the evening, and through the night,

"*It is better to Pray than to Rest.*"

As the good Moslem hears these words he leaves his work or his bed and obediently answers—

"*Here I am at Thy Call, oh Allah, here I am at Thy Call.*"

Down below us, as we lean over the crenellated walls of the gallery, lies the venerable sanctuary with its white domes and snowy roof, its great quadrangle and cloisters.

My guide Muhammed points out the different mosques within and without the city walls. The old tradition was that Kairwân contained five hundred mosques, but that is not so. About sixty mosques and over one hundred *Marâbouts*. The latter are simply the tombs of saintly Moslems, of whom an immense number came and still come to Kairwân to die, as it is supposed to be nearer heaven than most places. If Kairwân is nearer to heaven than the rest of the world, Muhammed and I must be much favoured, for we are certainly nearer to heaven at the top of this great *Minar* than any ordinary Kairwânis.

The view of the city and its surroundings is certainly one of the strange sights of this old-world continent. I was so struck with it that I must needs climb the *Minar* once more in the afternoon to gaze again upon the city and the plains beyond.

I could have gazed for hours on that scene,—the dazzling mass of white roofs and melon-shaped *koubas*, the crenellated walls girding the seven-sided city; the burnt-up country stretching for scores of miles to the north, even to the foot of the far-distant Zaghowân range, and here and there a white *Marâbout* where the saintly tomb stands out dazzling in the sun. Yonder is the faint track of the road leading toward Susa, along whose weary length yesterday we toiled. To the north, from the Bab el

Tunes, a track across the plain stretches away to the mountains, purple in the distance. The plain is brown and yellow, and more or less desert, though not approaching the brilliant golden hue of the Sahara near Tripoli.

Down below us we see the erratic, crooked streets, which, without definite purpose, seem to interlace the city; white terraces on the tops of the houses, where in the cool of the evening the Kairwânis sit to catch the slightest breeze. A figure here and there hurrying across a burning open space to get into the welcome shade again, camels moving out through the gates into the country, a train of donkeys with their drivers passing into the city—a few signs of life, but very few. Within it is almost like a dead city, while without the walls are tombs innumerable, ruined and uncared for.

I made Muhammed give me the names of the distant mountains, and I noted them down. On looking at a French map of the country I failed to identify any save the Ousselat range and the mountains of Zaghowân.

The story is told, and it is good as a story, that the French sent their officials through the country with instructions to ascertain the names of the rivers, mountains, ruins, etc. On the completion of the map, a very large proportion of the places were found to bear the name "*Ma'arifsh.*" The proportion was unnaturally large, and it was strange that ruins and rivers and mountains should all be called "*Ma'arifsh.*"

Yet all the explorers solemnly assured the authorities that upon addressing the natives out of their phrase-book in the set sentence, "What is the name of that place?" the Berber, or Zlass, or other Arab had replied, "*Ma'arifsh.*" These mountains and rivers and objects of interest were in fact all labelled with the interesting name (in Arabic) "Don't know." River Don't-know, the Don't-know Mountains, Oued Ma'-arifsh, Djebel Ma'arifsh.

It was late in the afternoon when we were able to enter the prayer-chamber of this great mosque of Kairwân, when the Faithful were returning home after due observance of the hour of prayer. Two soldiers guarded the great door, as from the fierce glare in the silent street I quietly glided in, leaving my shoes at the entrance. Through the great doorway I passed into the darkness of the many-pillared chamber, the Holy of Holies. Vast, weird, and dark as we entered, I felt a sensation of awe which almost chilled me. A *shaôush* flung back two of the many doors opening from the quadrangle and let in a flood of light upon the forest of marble, the stone floor with its many mats, and before me the holy spot, the *Mihrâb* directing the *Kibleh* towards the one city holier than Kairwân, great Mecca itself.

After the first sensation of awe had been overcome, one began to feel inclined to criticise. Looking round, there seemed, if anything, a want of height in this Djâma 'l Kebir, when its size is taken into consideration. It is in breadth something over eighty-five yards, and in length about forty yards (more than twice as broad as it is long). This great breadth is divided into seventeen aisles by rows of pillars—one central aisle, almost a nave, leading up to the *Mihrâb*, enclosed by two double lines of pillars, sometimes treble, and with eight aisles on either side. The height of the wooden ceiling cannot be more than thirty feet or so.

Of course in a mosque there is nothing upon the floor save matting; no seats or pews, or anything to detract from the height. The space above the arches is filled with arabesque plaster-work, not very striking. Upon the walls of the prayer-chamber may be seen the Arabic inscription, "*Cursed is he who shall count these pillars, for verily he shall lose his sight.*" And yet I counted those pillars, and found them to be two hundred and ninety-six in all.* Certainly my eyes smarted a good deal towards evening, and if it was not the glare of the fierce sunlight upon the white streets of Kairwân it must have been the effects of this pillar curse.

Two pillars much polished and standing close together attracted my attention, and I wished to polish them a little more by squeezing between them. It would have been satisfactory to have been able to do this, for the Muhammedan tradition is that

* M. Jacassey says that the number is one hundred and ninety-four (*Harper*, May, 1884). Perhaps the *genii* of the Sanctuary removed some pillars during his visit, or added some during mine.

he who passes between these two sacred pillars is safe for Paradise, for he thus proves his purity of soul. I suppose when very objectionable people try to pass through that the pillars close together and hold them tight, but for favoured persons such as myself, the pillars should open out a little, and the passage become easy. I approached the gorgeous *Mihrâb* niche, with its two red porphyry pillars* and lined inside with *lapis-lazuli* and shell-shaped designs in lovely marbles and mosaics. Here it is that the chief *Imaum* stands, taking "the eastward position" as he leads the devotions of the devout Moslems.

Then I moved forward and stood within the *Mihrâb* itself, and examined and touched the exquisite carving—stood actually on the holiest spot in Muhammedan Africa. One almost expected the mosque of Okhbah to fall and crush the infidel priest who polluted this holy spot by his presence. I was reminded of the words of Victor Guerin as to Kairwân (quoted in the first chapter), "Here the *Imaum*, interpreter and apostle of the Koran, has never found himself in the presence of 'un Ministre de l'Evangile.'"

Of course I was only here as a private individual;

---

* Mr. Rae says, "Hassan ibn Nouman, in the year 69 of the Hejra, embellished the Mihrâb, transporting thither the two superb columns, which still exist, of red stone marked with yellow stains, once taken from a Christian church, and for which the Byzantine Emperor had in vain offered their weight in gold" ("Country of the Moors," p. 295).

N

my mission to Kairwân was merely one of personal interest in this African centre of a strange religion. A lifelong training in the midst of this people would be necessary before a missionary could hope to do anything, and then he must be prepared to end a career, possibly of usefulness, and that very suddenly, at the hands of these fanatics.

To the left of the *Mihrâb*, close to the porphyry pillar on that side, is a large slab of white marble let into the wall and encircled by a broad band of green marble. It is a sort of memorial stone placed there by the founder of the mosque, El Sidi Okhbah ben Nafi, and bears some emblematic Moorish devices. Three huge chandeliers, each with some seven hundred olive-oil lamps, hang in the central aisle, and these are lit up on the Muhammedan feast-days. To the right of the *Mihrâb* is the *Membar* (pulpit).

The pulpit is elaborately carved in some very hard and dark wood. No two panels are alike; they are all perforated in fretwork till they look like wooden lace. Several of the panels under the stairs have bronze hinges and open outwards, showing receptacles in which books and rolls are kept. Close to the *Membar* is the *Maksoorah*, a sort of vestry, formed by a screen of the same dark carved wood, a retiring place for the *Bashi-Mufti* and the *Imaums*, and which encloses a considerable space at the east end of the mosque.

The two hundred and ninety-six pillars in the

prayer-chamber of the Djáma 'l Kebir are mostly Roman, the spoils of the whole of North Africa. One or two seem to have come from some very ancient church, for they have birds and flowers carved upon their capitals, figures of living creatures being forbidden to be made by Muhammedans. The character of these is considered ecclesiastical and Byzantine.* The capitals often seem to be fitted on to pillars which do not belong to them. Including the pillars round the quadrangle outside, the total of the pillars of this mosque is nearly five hundred.†

The great blemish and defect, to my mind, in the architecture of the Sidina Okhbah is, that it has been found necessary to strengthen the light Moorish arches by carrying beams of dark wood from capital to capital. This has too much the appearance of a temporary scaffolding.

In a paper read before the Royal Institute of British Architects, Mr. Herbert Carpenter has strengthened the theory already propounded by Mr. Rae ("Country of the Moors," pp. 296, 297), that this mosque was in the mind's eye of Kaliph Abd-el-Rahman III., the founder of the Mezquita of Cordova, when he planned that most magnificent structure.

* Several little details have been brought back to my mind on reading over Mr. Alexander Broadley's description of the interior of the prayer-chamber, and I must here acknowledge my indebtedness to him for many items of information.

† Here again is a divergence of opinion. Mr. Broadley says 439, Mr. Rae 435, and the French plan gives 501.

I have not visited Cordova; but I have often compared a photograph I possess of the interior of this mosque of Okhbah, with a photograph of the Mezquita in the possession of the Bishop of Durham at Auckland Castle. They are both taken from the same relative standpoints, and the views through those two groves of pillars marvellously correspond, and are eminently suggestive of one common design.

Mr. Carpenter considers that the Djâma 'l Kebir of Kairwân was the primitive model for mosques as far distant in the West and East as the Great Mosque of Cordova and the mosque of Azhar at Cairo. The latter was erected by General Gouher (or Jauher), the commander of the Kairwânis, who in A.D. 937 captured Fostat (Old Cairo), and founded a new city whose name should be like their own, "El Kahirah" (the City of Victory). The mosque of Azhar follows the general plan of the mosque of Kairwân.

Mr. Rae's statement that the original *Mihrâb* of Okhbah was covered up in 827 (A.H.) by Liadet Allah ibn Ibrahim, is, I believe, the authority of Mr. Carpenter for his theory that the present *Mihrâb* is not that of Okhbah. Mr. Carpenter considers that the present position of the first *Mihrâb* is within the entrance porch of the *Bashi-Mufti*, opening into the *Maksoorah*. The evidence, however, of the porphyry columns of Hassan ibn Nouman establishes the claims of the present *Mihrâb* incontestably, in my opinion.

May not Mr. Carpenter's theory be accounted for by an examination of the etching in the "Country of the Moors," in which the dome of the *Mihrâb* might be supposed to be a dome over the *Maksoorah?* Had Okhbah's *Mihrâb* been where he places it, the mosque must have been larger then than now. We have records of enlargement, but none of the reverse.

If Mr. Carpenter ever visits Kairwân he will, I feel sure, support me in my confidence that the present *Mihrâb* is the original *Mihrâb* of Okhbah.

I will close this chapter on Kairwân's chief mosque with an account, written by an Arab historian, of the choice of its position. "At the moment "when Okhbah was beginning the foundations of the "mosque there was a great division among the people "upon the subject of the choice of a site. Okhbah "had then during his sleep a revelation, and a voice "from on high addressed him thus: 'O thou beloved "one of the Master of the Universe, when the morning "shall have come, take the Standard, place it on thy "shoulder, thou shalt hear before thee a recital of the "*Tekbir* unheard by any but thee; the place where the "prayer will end is the spot chosen for the *Kibleh*, "there place in the mosque the holy niche for the "*Imaum*. The Most High God will protect this city "and this Mosque: His Religion will there be es- "tablished upon solid bases, and until the end of time

"there will the infidel be humiliated.' Okhbah awoke,
"deeply moved by such a Revelation ; he performed
"his ablutions and repaired to the place where the
"mosque should be, to pray. Soon a Mysterious
"Voice struck his ear; he followed It, and settled
"upon the spot where the Voice ceased as the site for
"the *Kibleh.*" *

* Translated from an article entitled "Kairouan, La Ville Sainte de la Tunisie" in the *Petit Almanach National de France*, 1882.

CHAPTER XVIII.

THE KAIRWÂNIS AT HOME.

An *aguz*—Imprecations—Hats and saddles—Cruelty to horses—Skin bazaar—Goats' horns—Buying carpet—*Hadadi*—Thunderstorm—African solicitor and English—Barbary barbers—*Fez* and *Sheshya*—Flies at lunch—Flocks and herds—The Renegade of Kairwân—Monk and Moslem—M. Soulie in *Figaro*—The Mahdi and Kairwân.

DISMISSING my escort, I roamed at large through the bazaars and streets of Kairwân, often taking notes when I could escape attention, but soon bringing a sullen angry crowd around me on attempting to sketch. An elderly toothless dame made a rush at me with clenched hands as I was sitting in one of the bazaars trying to copy some ironwork on a door. I anticipated a mobbing, when a Tunisian soldier in blue jacket and white trousers intervened and dragged her off.

"May Allah cut out thy heart, and make thy countenance cold." Impolite remarks of this nature did the *aguz* howl at me as the minion of the Bey tried to pacify her. She had seen that my head was not shaven.

Of course when a regiment of French soldiers is encamped outside the walls, and a company or so within the Kasba, the dangers of wandering alone amongst these fanatical Kairwânis are greatly diminished. Yet they hate the *Roumi* with a good solid hatred, increased materially since their subjection to the infidel army, the pollution of their mosques by the entrance of *Câfrs*, and the weight of a foreign yoke imposed upon the "City of Victory."

I felt that I must be careful, for if some raging *Marábout* flew upon me in order to gain Paradise and its *houris*, my little revolver with its six cartridges might be useless.

After wandering in the bazaars, I sat at length in an Arab *café*. The *caouadji* (coffee-house keeper) glided hither and thither in his bright turban, and reclining near the entrance I watched the decoration of the huge straw hats of the Djerid, nearly a yard across the brim, as they were being trimmed with scarlet or blue ribbons in fantastic patterns. These *Mvellah* are worn by the Bedouins and Moors in the country over their *sheshyas* or *tarbooshes*, and so there is allowance made for an immense head.

The next shop was full of brilliant trappings for the Arab steed. Saddles with high peaks before and behind, worked in *filali*—red morocco with green and gold ornaments. Everything about an Arab's horse is bright and picturesque, its head-gear of brilliant scarlet leather, the stirrups huge and quaintly ornamented.

STRAW HAT OF THE DJERID
ORNAMENTED WITH COLOURED TRIMMINGS.

Long and wide enough to hold the whole foot, they are sharpened at the corners, and with them the riders slash the poor creatures' sides, until they suffer dreadfully and have to be dressed on being brought in. The Arab in theory is devoted to his horse. But see him jerk the poor beast on to its haunches, or spur him with these razor-edged stirrups, and you begin to lose faith in the conventional Arab with his much-loved steed.

In the skin bazaar, Souk el Djulludin, an unpleasant odour was more than perceptible as the Moors dragged about freshly stripped goat and camel skins, shouting with all the power of their stentorian lungs the amount they are willing to sell at.

"Even so, even so, the hide of my brown camel for a trifle!!"

"Behold, oh thou, this valuable skin; in the name of the Prophet it is excellent!!"

I saw a pair of long horns on the skin of a silky black goat, and began to bargain for them to take home with me. The Arab impulsively took out a huge knife, and with a slash cut off the horns from the skin and gave them to me, never asking for any payment, but passed on crying out how much he would sell the skin for. I never quite fathomed that Arab's generosity, it was something so unexpected, and it often still puzzles me when I lean back in my chair and look up at those long horns from Kairwân.

There were very few of the celebrated carpets of the Holy City on sale in the bazaars. I was anxious to obtain one of these brilliant Moorish rugs, worked by the Kairwân ladies, and perhaps displayed my anxiety too plainly, for in consequence the Muhammedan shopkeepers professed great indifference as to whether they sold or not, and after unrolling the bright-coloured carpets, they speedily rolled them up again, as if the Eye of the Infidel might damage their brilliant hues. Nor was I at all anxious to buy at the price they suggested, and, much to their disgust (outward at all events), I proposed to give half of what was asked.

I sauntered away, and later in the day I came back, and sitting cross-legged beside an old Moor, had the carpets again displayed. It ended in my bearing off in triumph a brilliant rug, in which the prevalent hue is dark crimson, and upon it is richly worked arabesque patterns in violet and green, light blue and yellow.

There were a pair of maternal wrists at home that I wished to encircle with *Hadadi*—silver bracelets manufactured by the Bedouins. Cross-legged and patronising I sat in the little store of a stately Moor, on the dais open to the street, and as he had not what I wanted, the neighbours brought their goods to me, which I examined carefully, always looking at the silver mark attentively, just as if I knew something about it. They seemed to be impressed, and my behaviour evidently was a success. When I brought some gold out of my pocket, an unpleasant expression passed over the face of some in the crowd of onlookers, and I began to feel that perhaps fanaticism was not the only danger for a solitary infidel in Kairwân.

A strange darkness begins to overshadow the city, the blazing sun is obscured, and the heat becomes more intense, drops of moisture trickle off the brows of the Moors, and a distant grumbling tells of thunder. Down comes the rain in a solid sheet, an unexpected sight in June in the city of Kairwân. Seated at one of the entrances to the bazaars, I watch the scene without and within. Just outside across the street is a fountain and troughs for watering the cattle. A score of horses, mules, and donkeys are drinking and kicking, whinnying and biting, plunging and rearing, while their attendants are getting soaked through in the rain and are execrating everything in expressive Arabic. "Oh thou daughter of a naughty one, keep thy heels down." "Thou steed of Shaitan, wilt thou drink, and cease to bite my ass's ears?" "May Azraïl seize thee, O mare, if I chastise thee not."

I have taken my seat in front of a *Koodjah's* sanctum and (naturally) feel at home. I look round with interest in this African solicitor's office, and wonder if a certain valuable document with blue stamps, in which my name is prominent, would make him interested in the *Roumi* reclining upon his carpet. The legal gentleman, in snowy turban and scarlet *djubba*, encourages litigation in the minds of angry clients who sit cross-legged around him. Having received advice (to the extent of 6s. 8d. or thereabouts), they *salaam* and retire, and my "learned friend" passes from common law to conveyancing.

The store opposite is interesting. It is closed, when its owner is absent, by two folding doors, which meet longitudinally, and open upwards and downwards. The lower shutter comes down on the divan about a foot above the level of the street; the upper one, when fastened up, makes a sort of canopy above, from which hangs a short black iron chain with a ring. The portly Moor coming back from the mosque hauls himself up by this from the street into his throne, and then, seated amidst his goods, he looks for all the world like a Chinese mandarin in a josshouse, surrounded by piles of *henna*, pepper, beans, dirty green soap, whip-like candles, and other useful articles.

I buy some of these strange candles, and also invest in some *henna*, in order that any fair friends at home who wish to dye their finger-nails a bright carnelian hue may follow Oriental custom. I saw many Moors with their legs tattooed in fashion like the clocks upon stockings.

Until the rain clears off I sit and study Oriental costumes and customs. A crowd of Moors at the entrance present an interesting study, in scarlet *djubbas*, or chocolate and green. A tiny Arabette in blue rushes wildly after a young bird, which tries to escape, but is seized and borne off in triumph; another Mauresque infant in scarlet, with a somewhat faded, diminutive *sheshya*, gazes at the stranger in his flannels and strange black-leather boots, and fear seems almost overpowered by curiosity. He is warned by his elders, " Touch him not ; he is a ' cut-off' one."

An uncomfortably important gathering begins to make me the cynosure of neighbouring eyes, as I scribble notes in my pocket-book. Some of the onlookers, however, are amused to see me writing the wrong way—beginning at the left-hand side instead of the right, which every well-informed Moor knows is the only correct way of writing.

An Arab boy with a tray wanders by in the covered bazaar, carrying bun-like loaves of bread, vociferating as he sells to the shopkeepers a supply for their next meal, " Verily good bread and sweet ; oh, satisfy thy hunger." Yonder an Arab with one eye leads another who has none. A large number of blind people seem to live in Kairwân. They must have been trying to count the pillars in the Sidina Okhbah.

I wander through all the bazaars again and again, passing along the vaulted corridors, with shops on either side, each trade in its own section—one part devoted to yellow slippers, another to dry goods, another to woollen, cotton, silk, etc.*

* The description of the streets and bazaars given by my good friend Jacassey in *Harper* is so vivid that I cannot forbear quoting from it. "The small dilapidated shops are "two or three feet above ground, and are furnished with awnings "of boards, with matting at the sides, to protect them from the "sun. Open during the day, they are closed at night by a "large door as high and as broad as the shop. On one side "the tailors sit crouched, spectacles on nose, gravely plying their "needles, following with paternal eye some little children with "Semitic faces who gambol in the shop when they are not "occupied in winding skeins of cotton, or in reading in a shrill "voice from old greasy cardboard chapters from the Korân. "Elsewhere the braziers hammer those curious brass vases "whose original forms make them sought for as ornaments.

"Here others are polishing the long gun-barrels, and in-"crusting and damascening with arabesques the butt-ends of "muskets and blunderbuses. There still others are stitching "with silver and bright woollen threads saddles and game bags "and pieces of harness. Further on others are kneading cakes, "while near them are cooks tending the hot display of *merca* "(meat with sauce) and of *mergaz* (fried sausages), which they "sell by the portion.

"The first impression as one enters the bazaars is vague "and confused. From the narrow streets, crudely bright, one "passes under the dark arches, where objects can be dis-"tinguished with difficulty; where the side galleries open, the "light varies sharply in intensity. Sometimes a bright ray of "sun cuts the shadow like the flash of a Damascus sword, and "makes the millions of impalpable atoms sparkle in a golden "haze; then little by little the eye accustoms itself to it, and "one may admire at leisure the bits, the bridles, the velvet and "morocco saddles constellated with embroideries, the rare rich "stuffs woven with gold. . . . It is curious and amusing enough "to look about the shop of an Arab, and these good people "allow you to inspect everything, and, in order to detain you,

The storm has passed away, and already the ground is nearly dry under the scorching sun.

Buying a hatful of *mishmash* (apricots), I enjoy the luscious fruit and feel happier. In and out among the tortuous streets all over the city, and sometimes obtaining a momentary and interesting glimpse of an interior where carpet weaving was going on; I notice especially the ornamental work upon the doors of many houses, where the wood is studded with nails in pattern. It is strange to see the Sign of the Cross in a very central position in this rich arabesque ornamentation. It is quite prominent again and again, and this in the home of Muhammedan fanaticism.

"hospitably offer you coffee. The real charm of the bazaar is
"in contemplating the movement about one. The shops are
"surrounded with narrow stone pavements, two feet high,
"serving as a show place, between which are the roadways
"like little ravines. There, encountering and mingling with
"each other, are the cavalier, the frightened camels, the
"caravans of asses with their modest gait, sometimes loaded
"with bricks, filling the baskets attached to their pack-saddles,
"sometimes with wood or with fresh herbs.

"Immediately after the prayer of the *hasarr* (at three o'clock
"in the afternoon) the galleries of the bazaars become the
"theatre of an auction sale. It is then that the tumult becomes
"indescribable. One's ears are deafened by the various noises,
"and it is with the greatest difficulty that one succeeds in moving
"about. Kairwânese and nomads come to put up for sale
"carpets, coverlets, burnooses, made by their wives, and old
"gold and silver jewelry. They cry the prices with a deafening
"voice, meanwhile making the tour of the galleries, holding above
"their head the objects for sale, in order to attract attention."

The barbers' shops were amusing. I did not patronize them, but I often lingered as I went past and watched the Moors, unturbaned, having their heads shaved and their ears manipulated, while on the wall were little mirrors and razors.

The Moor has his forehead and back of his head shaved, but leaves a substantial lock of hair on the top of his head for the Angel of Death to carry him by to Paradise. The Aïssaouia usually have thicker bunches of long hair growing on the top of their heads, and when they are performing the rites of their confraternity, they jerk their heads backwards and forwards and this hair comes all over their faces.

The Muhammedans all wear upon their shaven heads a fez, in North Africa generally known as a *sheshya* or *chaciah*, while the better class wear under it a white cap, or lining, which preserves the fez in a clean state. The Constantinople fez is darker coloured and has a thinner tail than the Tunisian *sheshya*. In Tripoli and Tunis the tail of the *sheshya* is often dark blue, and the thick material of the cap is considered bullet proof. Perhaps the tail originated in the escape of the thick lock of hair through a hole in the *sheshya*.* Round the fez a score of yards of light gauzy material are wound to make the turban,

---

* It is said that Abu Hanifah wrote a treatise on the growth of this lock of hair, advocating it, in order that in battle the decapitated Moslem's mouth or beard might not be defiled by an impure hand (Burton's "Mecca and Medina," p. 159).

and then, to give an artistic finish to this head-dress, a flower is stuck just over the right ear, sometimes a rose, often a small bouquet.

Passing back from the Bab et Tunes through the city to the Bab el Djulludîn, I look in at the Kaid's house close to the latter gate, and see the rooms which the author of "The Country of the Moors" occupied during his visit to Kairwân the Holy. Sidi Muhammed el Mourabet, the governor of the city and of all Southern Tunis, is a descendant of the valiant Almoravides, once supreme in Spain. I leave the city by the great double gateway, outside of which two French sentinels stand, and return to the *Locanda*.

The flies of Kairwân and I have *déjeuner*, and the flies have a good time of it. About eighty disport themselves upon my plate as a rule, the others cluster upon different dishes and promenade my face and flannels. I can sympathize now with the Egyptians, for a plague of flies is very embarrassing; it is almost like living in a beehive. Flies in one's meat, flies rashly bolting up one's nose, flies committing suicide in one's coffee and endeavouring to see what one's eyes are made of, flies dancing upon one's hot face and climbing up one's sleeves. Doubtless they are determined to avenge the wrongs of the Tunisians upon my Infidel person.

After *déjeuner* I lean out of my lattice, looking out upon the great wall built of little light-brown

O

bricks. The sun pours down, and there is not the faintest trace of the heavy rainfall of the morning. But more is coming yet; the heavy clouds roll up threatening as the thunder mutters and growls; the rain is longing to fall. At last it comes down again upon the thirsty earth, and every one rejoices, though many a *Mugrebi* gets soaked to the skin.

As I write at my open casement I see a panorama of Oriental life. Here come the flocks and herds of a patriarch, the possessions of some well-to-do Moor. First twenty she-asses with foals; then a dozen lady camels, each with a dear little camelette running alongside; then great flocks of fat-tailed sheep and black goats innumerable; and lastly a score of great he-camels, grumbling at the wet and the thunder and everything, although they have no loads on their backs. Two or three sunburnt Arabs follow, with the hoods of their *djubbas* over their heads, and the whole caravan passes away into the country.

The rain ceases and all is dried up again. A little Arab girl comes by with bangles on her ankles, her face disfigured by the dark-blue tattoo-marks down her nose. She is rattling some coins in a little wooden basin, and soon she returns with something sweet in it, into which, after the fashion of *Roumi* children, she often dips her finger as she struts along in her bright dress.

Across the road, before some sheds where an old man and a donkey live, a dozen Moors sit engaged in conversation, and each is a perfect study. One with a crimson turban round his *tarboosh*, in which is placed (over the right ear) a lovely flower; yellow slippers, "handsome brown legs," white *sirawal*, and delicate saffron *haic* gracefully thrown over a chocolate *djubba*, rather open at the neck and trimmed with bright green, setting off a fine face, with a pointed black beard and dark eyes and eyebrows. Following nature in these countries, it is the male that is seen in gay plumage; the women of Kairwân go about hidden from sight in black *haics*. After all, is the cock or the hen the best dressed, the duck or the drake, the lion or the lioness, the peacock or the peahen? The men here put ladies at home completely in the shade. Even Parisian ladies would declare their toilette "*la plus adorable.*"

Readers of Rae's "Country of the Moors" will remember the interesting account there given of a certain French renegade whom the author met in Kairwân while still a sealed city. He had left his own country, broken his monastic vows, and sought in the retirement of this old-world city peace of mind in the strange faith of Islam. I made inquiries for him in Kairwân through the *Shaôush* Muhammed, and though I was not able to speak to him, he was pointed out to me, just entering a mosque.

My *Shaôush* pointed to a fairly tall dark Moor with bowed head, putting off his yellow slippers as he passed into a mosque built into part of the market, and hurriedly exclaimed, "*Le Français, voilà! voilà!*" It was only a momentary glimpse, but it was interesting to see one who in this nineteenth century would deliberately turn from Monk to Moslem and rest satisfied in his new faith. He is a most devoted Mussulmân, never omitting his due *rakaats* when the *Adzân* sounds from the many minarets of the Holy City. What a change from his life in the monastery of La Trappe! Can one understand any one giving up any form of Christianity for the faith of Muhammed? It was a terrible blow to "El Hadji Ahmed," as he is now called, when his former fellow-countrymen appeared as the conquerors of Kairwân. He had hoped never to meet again the inhabitants of the land he had renounced.

I was told that he often sits with other Moors sipping coffee when not engaged in his work of teaching the youths of Kairwân; and that on some occasions French soldiers on leave have come by accident into the same place for some coffee. They have been astounded on being addressed by a Moor not merely in good French, but in the language of one of high culture, accustomed to the most refined society. The account of his long interview with Mr. Rae is exceedingly interesting and should be read by all for whom such a career has any fascination.

The Parisian *Figaro* has put forward a very plausible story, the hero of which is, strangely enough, a Frenchman who has been living at Kairwân. It says that he has lately joined the Mahdi, and is now his right-hand man. One is tempted to think that it is our friend Achmet, though his previous history certainly does not correspond with that given by the *Figaro* as the record of M. Soulie's life. It certainly seems likely that El Sidi Achmet would link his fortunes with those of the Mahdi, and this he may have done since last June. Undoubted is it that communication is kept up between the confraternity of the Kadria, whose *záouia* is just within the ruined bastion, and the Soudâni Messiah, who belongs to that very order of Abd-el-Kadr el Ghilani.

Soon after the great battle of November 3rd last year, the Mahdi's emissaries arrived in Tunisia, and one of the first to receive the news of his triumph would be the solemn conclave of the Kadria, elated with a hope that the day was not far distant when the Infidel should be once more driven far from the sacred city, and El Mahdi should reign from the T to the T, from Tangiers to the Syrian Tripoli.

CHAPTER XIX.

ENCOMPASSING THE CITY.

How to spell Kairwán—The City of Victory—Thermometer, 140° Fahrenheit—Dying camel—*Booma*—Gate of Peaches or Greengages—French camp—The Mueddin with *my* flag—The Mahdi again—Abd-el-Kader el Ghelani—The *Kasla* or *Keshla*—Suburb Jibliyeh—The Zaouia Tidjania—Mosque of the Olive Tree—A *Khaukh*—Suburb Kabliyeh—A shrunken city—Sketching the Great Mosque—The sacred well and the greyhound Baruti.

THE name of this Holy City of Kairwán is spelt in many different ways by various authorities. The French—whom Colonel Playfair follows—have it *Kérouan;* Herr Glesser writes *Quayrouane*, Leo Africanus *Cairaouan*, Sir Grenville Temple *El Kirwân;* the Kairwánis themselves, according to Mr. Rae, pronounce it *Käyrawán*.

Its meaning, according to Dr. Shaw, is simply *caravan*, a place of meeting; but *Kahira*, victory, is more likely to supply the root of the word. Its present position is certainly a sad commentary on such a name.

As I mentioned in the opening chapter, Mr. Rae (in 1877) was the first to make plans of Kairwân and the Great Mosque—and at considerable personal risk. He had no compass, and was guided simply by the position of the *Mihráb*. In this only was he partly misled, for the *Kibleh* of the Djâma 'l Kebir turns more to the south than to the east, owing to some error in calculation on the part of Okhbah or his followers.* The Kairwânis, on seeing Mr. Rae in European costume calmly promenading round their walls and taking measurements and angles, were naturally incensed, and it is a wonder that he did not share the Marquess of Waterford's stoning. His plan is wonderfully correct † in most points, and would have been very useful to the French artillery (who carried copies of it), if the white piece of calico had not been waved from the great *Minar*.

I set off one day to walk round the walls, carrying with me a little pocket compass, and the book containing the plan. It was midday, and the heat was

* Nothing, however, will ever persuade the worshippers in Okhbah's mosque that he was mistaken in following the supernatural direction given by the cessation of the *Tekbir*. "The accuracy of the site of this Kibleh is regarded as such that the imâm—turning neither to right nor to left to allow for possible inaccuracy—turns direct to the Kibleh" ("Country of the Moors," p. 294).

† Mr. Rae measured the walls with his walking-stick, and gave 3500 yards as the result (including every projection); the French engineers gave as a total 3385 yards, but they did not include the extra measurement of the projections.

something beyond imagination, simply scorching, withering, fiery. All the Kairwânis were indoors for their *siesta*. I took my thermometer with me, and holding it in my hand it soon registered 140° Fahrenheit. This of course was in the sun.

Passing out by the Susa gate, known as the Bab el Djulludin, or Gate of the Skinners, I made my way to the north-east, passing the great enclosure where the deep underground cisterns lie covered up from the hot sun. I was interested to see what had become of the dead camel which had blocked the way for the *carosse* the other evening. There was scarcely anything of the carcase left; beasts and birds had speedily effected a removal of the mortal remains of the poor *djmil*. Strangely enough, there was another dying camel lying there, with a small pile of *hendi* before it, and the poor beast's sufferings were sad to witness. It must be a favourite place for the departure of camels' spirits—just as the Moors prefer to die within yonder walls.

From this point the walls run in a north-easterly direction for about eight hundred yards, being some thirty or forty feet in height. They are built with light brown bricks, each little brick an oblong four inches long. The walls are finished at the top with crenellations rising a couple of feet, each a foot apart.

A little distance from the walls are mounds of rubbish here and there, and now and again a drainage opening is seen in the walls.

Not a soul was to be seen; the sun was too much even for the Moors. A *booma* flew out of its nest in the wall, and being dazzled and blinded by the light, it could scarcely fly, and I gave chase, pleased at the idea of adding a Kairwân owl to my curiosities. The chase was not successful, and the *booma* regained its hole. I clambered up the wall and put my arm into the hole, but it was too deep.

The walls are much the same as far as the Gate of the Peaches,* half round towers standing out at regular intervals. Yonder, round a well, is an encampment of French soldiers, and under the great gateway of the Bab el Khaukh sentries stand in the deep shadow. From the Bab el Khaukh onward now to the end of this stretch of wall is about two hundred yards. Mr. Rae makes this side of the city bend rather more than it really does, for from the cisterns to the *Marábout* near the eastern extremity, the wall runs almost in a straight line. As I passed the camp considerable interest began to be displayed in my movements, and the French army developed a spirit of inquiry. My nationality was a difficulty to many of them, and some, I learnt, took me for a Turkish officer.

Passing under the eastern tower I saw the muzzle

---

* Broadley corrects Rae's translation, درخ *khaukh*, greengages. Rae is considered correct, however. براقة *durrákah* is peach proper; *khaukh* is the common term for both fruits.

of a cannon peeping out in a threatening way above me, but it did not go off; then, turning the corner, I began to skirt that portion of the wall which runs parallel to the Great Mosque.

A little way from the wall I sat down, and roughly sketched the great *Minar*, when the Mueddin came forth, waving my dark crimson flag, and with a discordant, ill-tempered voice seemed to abuse the Faithful for not coming to prayer more regularly. All around me the baked plains were burning hot; indeed, the ground was so heated that through my boots it almost scorched my feet.

Turning the northern corner, I passed down the north-west side among the ruinous graves that lie scattered all around.

Here is the great ruined bastion, and just within it is the lofty white dome of a *záouia*, which may yet become historical. When wandering through the narrow streets within, I looked with interest on the great copper-covered doors of this building, the head-quarters in Kairwân of the great confraternity of Abd-el-Kadr el Ghelani, to which Muhammed Achmet el Mahdi belongs, and with which he doubtless keeps up communication.* All the more important citizens of Kairwân belong to this secret society, and the successes of their victorious *confrère* and leader have elated them with the hope that they

* See article in *Pall Mall Gazette* by Mr. Broadley, last November, upon the Mahdi.

may yet drive the hated *Roumi* far from the walls of a city unpolluted for a thousand years by such presence.

Passing on along the walls, I came to the castle, here called the *Kasla*, or *Keshlah*, and not Kasbah. Here is another of the five gates into the city, the Bab el Kasla. Into the city certainly, but not directly, for first you must pass through the great courtyard of the castle, and then out again by a smaller entrance into the town. It is not used as a thoroughfare. In the Kasla were quartered French infantry, who seemed overdone with heat. A large cistern in the centre was used continually by the thirsty soldiers.

After inspecting the Kasla, I returned through the huge gates, and passing down the fifth side of the city, I entered the suburbs which extend to my starting-point (Bab el Djulludin). That which we now enter is Jibliyeh. It surrounds the market-place, where in the open air a fair is held on Monday mornings outside the Tunis gate. Here is another of the *Medressas* or Muhammedan colleges of Kairwân, that of the Záouia Tidjania, which leads the most liberal and free-thinking of the Moslem schools of thought. The wall here gives a greater bend than in Mr. Rae's plan, almost coming out at right angles after passing the Tunis gate, forming what may be called the fifth and sixth sides of the city.

All the way round the city, on the inside of the

wall, is a fairly wide terrace, four or five feet below the summit, so as to allow soldiers to stand and fire between the round-headed crenellations. The wall itself is on an average seven or eight feet wide. Past the next tower, and the wall almost runs due south past the new gate and the suburb of Kabliych. There is nothing striking about the Bab el Djedid, but nearly opposite, a little south, is the Mosque of the Olive Tree, whose strange Kufic characters Mr. Rae has correctly delineated.

Colonel Lyon Playfair did not seem to recognize this. In his subsequent "Travels in the Footsteps of Bruce" he probably saw another inscription, an inscription which I copied from the *zâouia* of the Aïssaouia in the Kabliych suburb, and which may also be seen, I believe, on other mosques. It runs thus—

Like the inscription on the Olive Tree mosque (which exactly coincided with Mr. Rae's copy) it is also in raised bricks, repeated upon each of the four faces of the *Minar*.

Six years ago, besides the five gates of Kairwân, Mr. Rae found three posterns through which one could pass by bending low and squeezing between two smoothly polished pillars placed in the wall. One only of these *Khaukh* now exists, opening into the Kabliych suburb. I passed through it, and found myself in the street which encircles the city inside the walls. I came out again through the *Khankhat* and continued my circumambulation.

A young Moor had been watching my movements for some time, as with note-book, plan, and pencil, I inspected the walls. I invited him to come and look at Mr. Rae's sketches, and I showed him the picture of the Great Mosque, whereat he was intensely delighted, and cried "*Malêh! Malêh!*" (Good!) The plan also interested him intensely, as he recognized well-known sites.*

---

* I cannot resist quoting the amusing account given by the author of the "Country of the Moors," of his circumambulation of these same walls.

"The appearance of an Infidel in his ordinary dress, with a "large sheet of paper, on which he was recording his measure-"ments of their venerated wall, caused dissatisfaction among "the people : and they began to collect round me. I had sent "Perruquier and one soldier to the silversmith's to get the "bracelets, the other soldier and the old barber remaining "with me. As we went on the Moors followed, not liking the "proceeding. First there was a crowd of fifty, then of a "hundred : finally I had a mob of a hundred and fifty march-"ing in silence on my heels. Whenever I halted, to make the "measurement from tower to tower or to take an angle, they "halted too. The whole thing was exceedingly funny.

"First went the old barber, then the soldier, then I, then the "mob. At a sudden pause they would almost run over "one another, and come crowding to look over one another's "shoulders, wondering what the tall lunatic in the Frank dress

So here I am back at my starting-point after about an hour and a quarter's progress round the walls of the Holy City. If one can bear the heat there is no time like midday for roaming at large and taking notes, for nearly all the Kairwânis are in their houses. This broiling heat is too much for even the most fanatically inclined Moslems. It would be difficult to raise a crowd. Eleven hundred years ago, if tradition is true, instead of being able to walk around the walls in an hour, more than three days' journey would be required; and children had to be labelled with

"was about. Every now and then came a murmur suggestive
"of the Arabic word for brickbats, and I still think that if one
"of them had picked up a stone, many more would have done
"the same. It seemed a droll thing to be marching round the
"walls of an old sacred city in Barbary, with a crowd of men
"about me, satisfied in their consciences that I had no right to
"be there, and yet none of them molesting me. The boys and
"youths were disposed to grow insulting.

   * * * * * *

"Here the crowd, who had fancied I would enter by the Gate
"of Skins, which would lead me to the Kaïd's house, began to
"think that I was not going to stop, but circumambulate the
"walls without end. They began to draw back and curse or
"insult me: and when I had gone fifty yards further they
"stopped and raised a cry, a kind of groan and yell in one,
"which their pent-up feelings gave a remarkable vigour to.
"This encouraged passers-by, and they too cried and hooted:
"*Kalb! Khansir! Kafir! Yahûdi!* There would have been
"no satisfaction in putting twenty or thirty to death where all
"were equally interested: and I reflected, too, that I had no
"special African evangelizing mission which would have justified
"me in making war on my own account—so I went tranquilly
"on, and terminated my labours where I had begun."

name and address in order that when lost they might be returned without delay.

I was anxious to obtain a sketch of the Great Mosque, and so entered the Bab el Djulludin, and passed along the inside of the wall. One can almost walk round the city inside the walls, though the road is blocked in some places by projecting walls. Near the Gate of Peaches I ran up some steps and stood on the terrace (about four feet wide) below the crenellations, and looked out over the heated plains, with their interminable gravestones, and saw the French soldiers encamped round the well. Being abused by a member of the French army for examining the fortifications, I maintained great self-control, and resolved not to make it a cause of an Anglo-Gallican Conference.

In the great space to the south-east of the mosque, I sat down on a stone and began a sketch of part of the true eastern side. Some low buildings between me and the mosque had to be ignored in order to get a pleasant view. Dark-visaged Moors began to watch the performance from different points, and children crept up to see what the infidel was doing. They ran off delighted when copper coins were distributed, and despite the scolding and threats of their parents, soon returned, crying "*Kif-kif.*" The crowd rapidly increased, but I soon had done all I wished, and moved on to sketch one of the Moorish doorways of the western side. Standing in a quiet corner, no one saw me for a little while, until a young Moor swinging his arms came by, and gave a shout of surprise. I should have been surrounded if I had not speedily pocketed my book and "moved on."

Parched with a consuming thirst under this glaring, burning sun, I made my way to the sacred well of Kafayât (or "enough"), on the eastern side of the mosque, near which I had been sketching. Some soldiers were drawing water, and they gave me a drink out of a *barâda*. This well, besides being sacred, is never failing, which is still more important.

A Sfaxine tradition says that the well was discovered in the days when Kairwân was a-building and its founders were parched with a consuming thirst. A greyhound belonging to Okhbah came in covered with mud, and the sagacious and considerate animal brought its master to this well, which thenceforward received its other name of Baruti, in memory of the dog.

That it communicates with the sacred Zemzem at Mecca is well known to every good Moslem, for did not a pilgrim drop his wooden platter with a coin nailed to the bottom into that holiest of wells, at the birthplace of the Prophet, only to find it floating in Baruti or Kafayât, as he journeyed home through Kairwân the Holy?

My faithful Chicco has entirely disappeared, but I live in the hope that he will appear according to compact upon the fourth day. M. Victor Guerin tells us that pilgrims come to Kairwân to get "steeped in the spirit of Islamism." I trust my thirsty little Maltese will not be found to be steeped in a more material spirit when the time comes for us to leave Kairwân and its strange charms behind.

CHAPTER XX.

SAINTLY RESTING-PLACES.

Three hairs from Muhammed's beard—Tomb of the Companion—Fanaticism—The hours of prayer—*Beni Yssou*—Son of a gun—The anchors of Noah's ark—Reduction of Sebastopol by Kairwân muzzle-loaders—Sacred swords—Sunday in Kairwân—Worshippers in the Great Mosque.

MUHAMMED was waiting for me when I returned from my circular tour, for he had arranged for a visit to two very interesting tomb-mosques. One is that of "My Lord the Companion" (of the Prophet)—Abdullah el Belawi; the other of a modern and warlike saint who was fond of anchors and cannon balls, the Emir Abada. The former is about half a mile north-west of the city, and can be seen from that camel track which is known as the Tunis road. Once more through the city; in at the Tanners' Gate, along the main street, past the Ferik's house, and the bazaars, through the Bab et Tunes, and so out on the plain again.

Here we walked through part of the necropolis of Kairwân—grave-stones with turbans carved at the top, grave-stones without, broken, ruined, marble-slabs with ancient inscriptions, a veritable Gehenna of Kairwân. Half a mile across the mounds we saw a square pile of white buildings baking in the fierce glare. A square *Minar* rises above them with brilliant tiles, like dragon's scales, on its sides and roof. As we approached we saw a Moorish gateway and a courtyard within enclosing a mosque.

This is the resting-place of "My Lord the Companion," he who sleeps with a hair of the Prophet's beard upon each eye and on his tongue.* From this circumstance a popular and erroneous idea has prevailed that he was the barber of Muhammed. The French still call the building the *Mosquée du Barbier*. The name of this ancient saint, it is well to remember, is simply Sidi Abdallah Ben Wadib el Belawi, Saib en Nabi. Sidi is the ordinary title given to a superior; Abd-allah, the slave or servant of God; Ben Wadib, the son of Wadib the Belawite; Saib or Sahib, the companion; en Nabi, of the Prophet.

The magnificence of this building far surpasses anything else to be seen at Kairwân, while its sanctity

* M. Jacassey quotes the legend thus: "Sidi Sahib followed the Prophet in all his expeditions, and lived under his tent. One day, when the Prophet was being shaved, Mohammed gave him three hairs from his beard—inestimable relic, which the believer religiously preserved all his life. He came finally with Ogbah to Kairwân, where he died. Then following his instructions, they placed one of these hairs on his tongue, and the other two on his eyes" (*Harper*, vol. lxviii. p. 850).

is as great as, and by some considered greater than, that of the Djâma 'l Kebir.

Passing through a Moorish archway out of the glare, we entered an exquisite vestibule, with tiled walls and floor, and vermilion ceiling. Thence, through several Mauresque chambers until we found ourselves in an open court, into which the sunlight blazed, while round it in deep arcading ran a pillared cloister. It seemed like an arabesque fairyland. I stood almost breathless and gazed up at the richly carved ceiling of the cloisters, the white marble pillars, the black-and-white Moorish arches, the brilliant tiles reaching high up the walls, the snowy Mauresque designs above.

Dark and sullen stood the guardian of the shrine, showing his strong feelings in an unmistakable manner while Muhammed exhibited the Ferik's firman. Slipping off my shoes and following these two Moslems in their flowing graceful robes, I passed down the cloisters until I stood opposite the entrance to the Tomb of the Companion. Before passing in to the chamber where he lies, I noticed a stone let into the wall, with Arabic inscriptions, which tell of the last governor of Kairwân and of the Sheikh el Esran, a Muhammedan writer who lies buried here near the "Companion."

In a room hard by is also the catafalque of a Hindoo pilgrim of great sanctity, known as Abdullah ben Sherif, who died here in the last century.

At last we stood before the entrance to the tomb, while the unhappy janitor unwillingly opened the door. It swung in a huge marble doorway, with a window on either side, evidently of Italian sculpture, finished above in richly carved fruit and flowers. The mosque, though built about A.H. 70, has been repaired and practically rebuilt several times since then.

We now passed into a chamber where few Christians have ever stood, and I beheld the very Tomb of the Companion. Small stained windows of thick bull's-eye glass shed a dim light, while fumes of incense hung heavily on the air. A great catafalque takes up a large proportion of the chamber, and round it a bronze lattice supported at the corners by marble pillars. Over the catafalque rich palls are laid, heavily brocaded, the upper one—green velvet embroidered with silver thread—being given by the Bey. Above are hung many brilliant banners, also ostrich eggs and large gilt balls of earth from Mecca. (The symbolism of the latter, I saw suggested somewhere is the gullibility of the Faithful, who can swallow anything.) Gorgeous thick carpets cushion the floor, the ceiling rises in a dome of exquisite carved work, and from the centre hangs a large glass chandelier.*

We passed out through other richly ornamented

---

* See accounts given in "Tunis, Past and Present," and in article "Kairwân" in *Harper*, May, 1884.

chambers, and as I went through the door I offered the fanatically sour-looking Moor some money. He threw it down as if it had burnt him, but subsequently I saw him picking it up. It could not have been that it was not enough. As we passed out through the gate we were cursed by some Moorish women at a lattice casement in one of the buildings, who cried after us with shrill piercing voices. I have not felt any the worse for it, but it must have been rather emphatic to have made Muhammed look solemn and walk hurriedly away.* Round this Tomb of the Companion is a *Medressa* or seminary of Mussulmâns, one of the Kairwân colleges for the promotion of fanaticism.

We entered the city once more, only to pass out again into the suburb Jebliyeh by the Bab el Djedid, or New Gate. The Kairwânis are outwardly very religious; one sees them streaming into the mosques at the hours of prayer. An old Moor gathered up his garments as he passed me, for fear my touch should render him ceremonially unclean. The hours of

* The Kairwânis will never lose their fanaticism. Some of them seemed to be misled by my costume and *sheshya*, but now and again quite unwittingly one provoked some good follower of the Prophet. M. Jacassey, too, had similar experiences. He says, "But the scene changed when I arose to mingle among the groups: the naked children who rolled themselves in the dust fled at my approach with frightful shrieks; the mothers took refuge under their screens, hiding their face in their hands, and the men glared upon me with wild and hostile looks" (*Harper*, May, 1884).

prayer are five: (1) Before sunrise, (2) at noon, (3) before sunset (about 3 p.m. generally), (4) during the twilight, (5) when night has set in. The Mueddin cries, "It is better to pray than to rest," and the seventeenth *Sura* of the Korân enjoins the faithful thus: "Regularly perform thy prayer at the declension of the sun, at the first darkness of the night, and the prayer of daybreak; for the prayer of daybreak is borne witness unto by the angels."

Kairwân is the head-quarters of the Muhammedan confraternity of the *Aïssaouia*. This name is variously explained. Mr. Broadley and others simply find in it a name for the followers of a Moroccne named Muhammed Ben Aissa, of Mequinez, while Dr. Tristram is amongst those who consider that it means "Sons of Jesus," Beni Yssou, and finds these devotees trusting in a text of the Nazarene Korân (Luke x. 19), "Behold, I give unto you power to tread on serpents and scorpions, and over all the power of the enemy, and nothing shall by any means hurt you."

Many Muhammedans belong to the Aïssaouia, which is an intensely fanatical form of Islamism. On certain occasions (at Tripoli on the *Marábout* day) they seem to lose their senses and to act like wild beasts. My friend Abdullah ben Said, Miss Tinne's servant, quiet and dignified as he generally is, rushes about on these occasions in the wildest fashion, *sans* turban, jerking his head about till the thick lock of hair covers his face. When in this excited state they will tear to pieces a live sheep and devour it, will cut themselves with swords, and feed pleasantly on the highly indigestible prickly pear.

The special correspondent of the *Times* (Mr. Broadley) wrote in that paper an account of some Aïssaouian revels which took place at their *záouia*, a few doors from the *Locanda* where I stayed, and which description also appears in his book on Tunis (pp. 183, 184).

A mosque with six melon-shaped domes rises above the Jibliyeh suburb, not very far from the *záouia* of Sidi Ben Aïssa. It is the tomb of the Emir Ben Said Bou Muphteh, or Emir Abada. This amusing old Moslem lived about thirty years ago, and seemed to have such power over the then Bey that he got anything done he wished.* He wanted seven domes put on his mosque, but only six were finished when the Bey died. He had four huge anchors carried for his delectation from Tunis and laid close to his house. Probably they had belonged to some man-of-war, and had been slipped hurriedly owing to weather or stress of circumstances. Yet now they are undoubtedly the very anchors which held Noah's ark to Mount Ararat! Their transport, Mr. Broadley tells us, employed five hundred Arabs during five months. We further read (in " Tunis Past and Present "): " During the siege of " Sebastopol, Amir Abada constructed two cannons " with his own hands. He wrote to the Bey that the

* " Tunis, Past and Present."

"Prophet had appeared to him and announced that on "their arrival before the beleaguered town the latter "would at once surrender. They were expeditiously "forwarded to Tunis, and, at the Bey's pressing request, "the Sultan sent a ship to convey them to Constanti-"nople, and thence to the Turkish camp before "Sebastopol. By an extraordinary coincidence, "within a few hours of their being landed the town "capitulated" (p. 174).

The tomb of this Conqueror of Sebastopol is very plain inside. Round the domes run Moorish inscriptions, and on the walls are huge boards painted black, with yellow lettering in Arabic, and containing whole *Suras* from the Korân. At the foot of the catafalque are three iron shells (nothing in them), and some cannon balls at the head. Upon the wall are colossal swords of great thickness. I took down one and found it fearfully heavy and of no use, as its edge was as blunt and thick as my finger. This was the armoury whence M. Galea obtained the specimen that I was shown at his house, the vice-consulate of Susa. The blades are covered with closely written inscriptions. A prophecy was made concerning these swords, that so long as they remained in Kairwân it should never be invaded.

Passing out through the nave-like entrance we met some Moors coming in to pray, and they scowled uncomfortably at the Infidel who so persistently invaded their sacred places.

It is Saturday evening, and scorched and tired I fall asleep very quickly on my rude pallet, and neither voice of Mueddin nor the tom-tom of Arab concert can awaken me, until the daylight streams in again at the dawning of the second Sunday after Trinity. For the first time I yearn a little for the country, where to-day it can be said—

"Calm is the morn without a sound."

I sit at the open casement reading the lessons for this Sunday, the histories of Deborah, Barak, and Gideon. Now all seem so natural as they are read in an Oriental light. One's surroundings here in wild Kairwân would furnish living pictures for many a sacred story.

Writing letters home, reading my Bible and "In Memoriam," the time soon passes. I stroll out through the busy streets, alone in the crowd, and as the afternoon passes, once more I draw near the Djâma 'l Kebir.

The great door of the prayer-chamber is open, and I stand silent and motionless, gazing on the scene within. It is the hour of prayer, and in the semi-darkness of the interior the stately Moors in their snowy dresses lift up their arms, saluting the Omnipotent, their God and mine, or falling on their knees prostrate themselves in adoration, touching the ground with their foreheads.

Listen to the words that many of them were

uttering—" In the Name of the Most Merciful God. "Praise be to God, the Lord of all creatures; the "Most Merciful, the King of the Day of Judgment. "Thee do we worship, and of Thee do we beg as-"sistance. Direct us in the right way, in the way "of those to whom Thou hast been gracious; not of "those against whom Thou art incensed, nor of "those who go astray."*

Most impressive was the scene, the bright sunlight reflected from the white houses behind me, and falling on the interminable rows of marble pillars and on those white-robed devoted Moslems all intently absorbed in their worship, until they rise murmuring, "*Allahu-ach-Kebar*" (God is most great).

Here in Kairwân the Christian may learn a lesson which the collect for this Second Sunday after Trinity emphasizes, " Make us to have a perpetual fear and love of Thy Name." The Name of God is indeed had in reverence by the followers of the Prophet, and they could pray the words of that collect of Gelasius most heartily to-day, though, alas! they could not, as we can, hopefully and trustfully offer the petition in the Name which is above every name, " through Jesus Christ our Lord."

* This is *Al Fâtihat*, the prayer offered on all occasions; it is to be found in the first *Sura* of the Korân.

CHAPTER XXI.

IN BEDOUIN-LAND.

Farewell to Kairwân—Drive through the Sacred City—Out on the desert plains—The mirage—A well at last—Bedouins and backsheesh—Dr. Tristram's experiences in Tunisia—Supper with the Waregrans—Bedouin hospitality and insect life—El Menarah—Beer-el-Buwita.

" UP with the Mueddin " might be the Oriental equivalent for a certain homely proverb. The first *Adzân* was echoing from the minarets as I rose on this my last morning at Kairwân, and soon was strolling through its sacred streets, already filled with early-rising Kairwânis. Returning to the *Locanda* at six, I found the four horses engaged in biting one another and whinnying defiance, and my Kairwânic treasures were being loaded.

After settling with the rascally owner of this *Roumi-fondouk*, we were ready to start, our water-jar was replenished, and with Arabic expletives the steeds were urged into their best pace. The Tunis gate lay at the far side of the city, and so we either must drive around the walls, through the Kabliyeh and

Jibleyeh suburbs, or boldly drive into the city and cross it to the Bab et Tunes. Sufficiently good reasons were shown to Chicco why we should do the latter, and emulate the example of the Gallic conquerors in their triumphal march through the Sacred City.

In a moment or two we were clattering through the deep archway of the Bab el Djulludin and meeting no opposition we trotted safely past the Caid's house. Chicco never uttered a sound as he urged the horses along the winding street, where the Kairwânis left their work in surprise and rushed out to see an "Infidel" driving through Kairwân the Holy. Here was a *Câfr*, a *Kelb-ibn-Roumi*, seated amidst his luggage in a Frankish *carosse*, rattling over the sacred stones. Some few turbaned friends could not but laugh as I touched my *sheshya* politely, putting on my best smile, but others scowled and turned back to their work muttering.

For the last time now through the great walls, under the Saracenic Bab et Tunes, and out into the busy market, *foum-el-bab*—without the gate, where the Monday fair was being held. Out on to the hot plains for our hundred-mile drive as we left the city of Okhbah behind, and turned our faces northwards.

Away we went over the treeless plain, bumping, rocking, and rolling, ever keeping the purple Zaghowân mountains before us to the north. Lizards darted over the burning sand, gigantic black beetles gazed up at us with amazement, while ants rushed hither and thither on the path of duty. Bedouin encampments were seen now and again, camels grazing on some scanty herbage, and little brown children chasing across to intercept the *carosse* in the hope that the *Roumi* would prove beneficent.

After about an hour I turned to look for the last time at Kairwân the Holy. Far away behind us the city walls stood out white in the fierce blaze of the morning sun, the *Minar* of the Djâma 'l Kebir rising above all, like a Mussulmân *santon* guarding the African plains; an outward and visible emblem of the spiritual domination of El Islam. How different were my feelings as I looked back upon those white walls and upon my experience within them, when compared with the sensations which possessed me last week, as from Sidi el Hani I first saw Kairwân in the extreme distance, the evening drawing on. No longer mysterious and dreadful, shrouded in uncertainty, steeped in fanaticism, but almost homely and familiar; containing many friendly Moors and copper-loving children, the awful Djâma 'l Kebir as familiar as Westminster Abbey, the sealed city now unsealed to me, the last intact Moorish sanctuary invaded by a *Roumi Imaum*.

One hundred miles of Bedouin-land to be traversed—great plains sometimes perfectly desert, sometimes a little cultivated in patches of barley, or flaming with great bushes of oleander. At first it was desert, barren desert. Not the brilliant Sahara-gold of the interior, but a dun-coloured expanse, on which tufts of coarse *halfa* grass and stunted tamarisk bushes were scattered, and strange ribs of dark rock jutted up through the soil like the vertebræ of some monstrous endless serpent.

Not many hours had passed before I saw a sight always linked in one's mind with the desert—the *mirage*, and this steadily kept before us through the fierce heat of the day. Away on our "port bow," a silvery line stretched along for about one-fifth of the horizon. It grew into a lovely calm lake, a veritable *sebka* or *shott*, with trees upon its farther bank, and a white felucca sail which seemed to skim its surface. The thirsty horses, covered with impalpable white dust, and scorched beneath the blazing sun, pricked up their ears and quickened for awhile their pace, but still the lake kept ever ahead, or far away to the left. One could discover by gazing intently that the trees upon its farther bank were rocks apparently floating in the air, and the felucca sail was part of the roof of a saintly Muhammedan tomb drawn up into this silvery phantasy produced by the fierce heat.

Through the heat of the day the mirage appeared, sometimes in one part of the horizon, sometimes in another, until we became quite used to it. After journeying for four long hours from Kairwân, we drew near to a well, an event indeed on the Sahel. The poor horses strained and struggled as they sniffed the water, and were all painfully eager for the first drink.

Poor Chicco lost his temper and spluttered with rage as the four heads all tried to get into the one bucket which we carried. How loathsome the water was! It smelt horribly; none but horses could touch it. I suffered dreadfully from thirst, my mouth became dry and harsh, and for hours I could not get a drink, for the water we had brought with us was almost as vile as the awful liquid found in the wells, and these were some twenty miles distant from each other.

A hum of insect life went up as we rested a little —dragon-flies innumerable, and from the tamarisk bushes the cry of the cicala.

Half a mile from us a great flock of black goats walked before a Bedouin shepherd, who stalked along with his crook in his hand. The goats trotted in front with their perky black tails on high, but the sheep followed the shepherd. It is true in the East that "they know his voice and are known of him."

An hour later we were rather embarrassed by the appearance of a dozen Bedouin horsemen, who rode down on us in the hope of getting some money. They were mounted on fiery little Arabs, with coloured saddle-cloths and huge cruel stirrups, and their white *haics* flew gracefully in the wind. Some of them wore the huge straw hats of the Djerîd, and strange objects many of them looked with their faces scorched into an inky, dirty black. They rode round us shouting at Chicco and the *Roumi* in white, and could easily have obliterated us from animated creation on that great lonely plain. I was thankful when at last they all trotted away, some laughing, some displaying gleaming white teeth as they gave us a final scowl.

There is not much danger in Tunisia now; the country is comparatively quiet, though Europeans are occasionally attacked by the Arabs.* If, however, several Englishmen travelled together, they would be practically safe. In past years there was considerable danger in travelling in Tunisia, but now it is somewhat minimized, or I might have found it more difficult to get home from Kairwân.

Dr. Tristram told me, one evening after my return, the interesting story of his adventures in 1857, when he travelled in the interior of this country. One is sorry that he has not had time to publish his journals. Here is one of the incidents of his journey. One evening, as his party were approaching the Algerian frontier after a long fatiguing day, they suddenly came upon the black tents of a *douar* of Waregrans, one of the most dangerous of the border tribes.

Dr. Tristram's party consisted of himself and two

* The following telegram appeared in the *Daily News* of November 14th, 1883:—"Four European merchants travelling from Gallipia to Tunis have been assaulted by Arabs. One of the Arabs having attempted with a dagger to wound one of the merchants, the latter shot him with a revolver. The Europeans then fled to Menzil Temim, where they asked assistance of the governor. He having heard that the whole tribe was in revolt answered that he had not sufficient force to protect them."

English friends, some five or six servants, with horses and mules. Their party, however, had been increased by a score of hangers-on—disaffected Tunisian Arabs, who sought to cross over to Algeria as the attendants of *El Roumi*.

They were all sinking for want of water, and upon seeing the Arab encampment, were overjoyed at the prospect of quenching their thirst, not knowing at first that they were Waregrans. The Bedouins refused to give them any water, and professed that they were about to move away to some spot where water could be had, and that they had none for themselves. This was palpably a lie.

The English party did not carry a tent, and they eventually succeeded in persuading the Waregrans to pitch one for them. They refused to supply them with any refreshment, however, and would not eat " bread and salt " with them, but suspiciously watched every movement in the English camp. The solitary tent of the *Roumis* was pitched upon a slope of the *wady*, on the opposite bank to the Waregran *douar*.

Wandering gradually away from his tent, Dr. Tristram roamed about with an Arab attendant, seeking water. Suddenly they came upon a Bedouin boy from the enemy's camp tending cattle. He was promptly seized, and, before he knew what had happened, was safely gagged with a smooth stone and a pocket handkerchief. The lad, who knew nothing of the arrival of the *Roumis* at the camp, and who perhaps had never seen a white man before, was petrified with horror.

With a pistol in one hand, and a Spanish dollar in the other, Dr. Tristram told him to lead them to the nearest water, and he would be rewarded with one or the other as he was refractory or compliant. The lad soon brought them to a delicious spring, where they quenched their thirst, and filled some vessels they had with them. Returning quietly to the tent, they walked their beasts away at intervals as if for pasture, but brought them all circuitously to the spring.

Darkness came on, and Dr. Tristram and his two friends retired to their tent to rest, but noticed that across the *wady* all the Arabs were sitting sullenly in front of their tents, watching every movement in the *Roumi* camp.

The moon arose, shining brightly upon the Waregran encampment, but leaving the interior of Dr. Tristram's tent in darkness. The Arab sheikh and two chief men came and sat in front of the *Roumis'* doorway, as if for conversation. Dr. Tristram and his friends wanted rest, and became wearied of answering the Waregrans' questions, so, lying down with their guns in their hands, one watched while the others in turn slept. They had been asleep a short time, when one of his friends touched Dr. Tristram and whispered to him not to move much, but that one of the three Waregrans had stolen his pistol, and, with the other two, was examining it. As they looked out into the moonlight there were the three Waregrans trying in vain to work the repeating revolver—a strange weapon to them.

Rising quietly, the three Englishmen covered the three Bedouins with their guns, and cocked their triggers, causing them to start. They were all completely cowed as the three long barrels glistened in the moonlight, a few feet before them. Quietly the Arab who had taken the pistol brought it back, and, entering the tent, returned it with thanks to its owner. He was instantly pinned to the earth and a barrel pressed to his forehead. "Order supper for us at once or you shall die." He swore by the Beard of the Prophet that he would, and was as good as his word. They all supped bravely on *kous-kousoo* provided by the Waregrans, and having tasted the Arabs' food were safe.

"It was the will of Allah that we should either sup over you or with you. It is *Kismet*."

So the travellers, their attendants, and hangers-on, all had enough and were well filled. Next day the difficulty was to escape. As long as they remained in sight of the place where they received hospitality they were safe, but once away from that spot the Waregrans might do anything they chose without violating the Arab tradition. Dr. Tristram's account of their strategic departure was as intensely interesting as the history of his other Tunisian adventures, and though his life has been in his hand again and again in the East, he considers that his adventure with the Waregran bandits brought him nearest of all to a sudden death.

During this digression concerning the Waregrans the reader may imagine us as having got rid of our troublesome Bedouins, and toiling on mile after mile over the blazing plains, gradually approaching the Zaghowân mountains, with their quaintly shaped summits and boldly defined strata.

After seven weary hours' of very heavy driving we left the more desert land and found ourselves in a comparatively fertile country, between the mountains and the Mediterranean. We approached another Bedouin *douar*, with its black goat-hair tents, passing a scanty crop of waving barley, in the midst of which wandered several pensive donkeys. I called a halt for refreshment, and making obeisance, touching forehead and heart as I bowed, entered one of the tents with the permission of its owner, saluting the Arabs with the "*Salaam alicûm*" ("Peace be with you"). The Bedouins received me, and I reclined on a piece of esparto matting while they prepared coffee and boiled some eggs.

A little brown child with bangles on its ankles sprawled about on the floor. A hole in the ground was the fireplace, and the smoke, after making efforts to destroy insect and other life, escaped as best it could, mostly through the doorway. All around sat and reclined brown, savage-looking Bedouins, more or less unclean, conversing more or less in a shout, their animated conversation (aided greatly by violent gesticulation) chiefly relating to the stranger who had come and taken up his quarters in their tent.

The women returned from the neighbouring well, bearing their huge stone jars on their shoulders. They were gracefully dressed in a loose flowing piece of blue linen, with a reddish handkerchief on the head; their dark faces fringed with coins, which hung also on their breasts; their eyes were darkened; their faces stained with henna, or tattooed slightly; and they wore huge ear-rings, fastened to their hair, being too heavy for the ear alone to carry.

Now and again an Arab horseman dashed into the encampment on his fiery steed with brilliant saddle-cloth, and drawing rein suddenly, leapt from his horse and disappeared into a tent.

A huge negro, the attendant or slave of the chief man, brought me an immense bowl of curds, "butter in a lordly dish," and was quite gratified by my partaking of it, scorning the idea of remuneration. Our horses were being refreshed meanwhile, and soon we bade our Bedouin friends farewell, leaving a present behind.

Through the afternoon, on and on over the treeless plain, sometimes descending suddenly into a dry *wady* or river bed, and then painfully scrambling out at the other side. Signs of agriculture became frequent, and the creaking *siniehs* here and there were yielding gushing streams from the great skin-bag, as camel or ox descending the inclined plane drew up the precious water.

The mountain range to the left acquired quite a Dolomitic character, and about three o'clock we were abreast of the "Three Sisters" with their strange-looking summits.

Towards the end of the afternoon (about ten hours from Kairwân) we approached a very interesting Roman ruin. A stone-faced building, in shape like a gigantic straight-sided barrel set on end, it had huge projecting bands at intervals of five or six feet all the way up. It was a squat tower, in height perhaps sixty feet, and about thirty-five feet in diameter.

I find that Dr. Shaw says of it: "Two leagues from Hammamet is the Me-narah, a large mausoleum, nearly twenty yards in diameter, built in a cylindrical form, with a vault underneath it. Several small altars (supposed by the Moors to have been formerly so many *menara, i.e.* lamps, for the direction of the mariner) are placed upon the cornice and inscribed with the names of

L. AEMILIO AFRICANO AVVNCULO C. SVELLIO PONTANO PATRVELI. VITELLIO QVARTO PATRI."

I left Chicco, and walking across to the tower, made a rough sketch from the west side, where the view was nearly perfect. Fragments of stone lay all around—the ruins of some considerable buildings. An Arab shepherd was feeding his flock of fat-tailed sheep under the shadow of the tower, camels were browsing in the scorching sun, and *cicalas* buzzed around. The Bedouin curs growled and showed their teeth, as their owners suspiciously watched me with my note-book. In the distance the *carosse* was creeping on over the plain, and far, far away to the east the blue line of the Mediterranean stretched northwards to the white houses of Hammamet, the Town of Wild Doves, circling round the bay.

We were near the end of our day's journey, after fifty-five long miles over the burning desert plain and camel track. For eleven long hours, which under that sun seemed like days, we had jolted and rolled, and Chicco had poured forth expletives until his mouth was parched. At last, passing along one of the finest hedges of prickly pear I have ever seen, some fourteen feet high, we entered a white archway, and found ourselves inside an Oriental caravanserai, a Tunisian *fondouk*.

BEDOUIN.

CHAPTER XXII.

A NIGHT IN A KHAN.

The African traveller at Bir-el-Buwita — Fellow-travellers — Bedouin camp fire — Insect horrors — A British subject — *En route* to Tunis — Barley harvest — El Khwin — Kroumbalia — Hammam el Enf — Thascius Cyprianus — A Simoon — The fire-horse — Camel dumpling — Farewell to Bedouin-land.

THE last night of 1849 was a memorable one for the great African traveller Barth, and also for a certain Arab caravanserai in Tunisia called El Bir-el-Buwita, which being interpreted is "The well of the little cupboard."

Henry Barth was setting out on his five years wanderings in the interior of this "Dark Continent," and upon the second day from Tunis, December 31st, he arrived at this spot. He writes, "I shall never forget this the last night of the year 1849" (Travels, vol. i. p. 2). At midnight, as the new year of 1850 came in, Barth and his fellow-traveller Richardson exchanged congratulations and good wishes, in which they were joined by their Muhammedan servants.

Perhaps "Abd-el-Kerim," as he was known by the

Arabs, occupied the same little grated room which, upon a midsummer night in 1883, was occupied by a less distinguished visitor. It was very interesting to come across a *fondouk* with such associations, to find one's self in the Bir-el-Buwita of Barth.

The caravanserai stands on the Sahel, some miles away from any building or village, the nearest being at Hammamet, on the shores of the Mediterranean. It is a two-storied white building, with an arched entrance through which the camels and the country carts pass into the courtyards in the rear. There was accommodation for three classes of travellers: the Bedouins, with their camels and donkeys, went into the furthest courtyard, a colonnaded quadrangle where, under the shelter of the pillared cloister, they collected in groups or lay down for the night with their beasts. The second-class travellers, consisting of a few Tunisian Moors, stayed in another courtyard, nearer to the main building, and hired one of the stables which surrounded this quadrangle, paying a few pence for the luxury, and in the warm weather leaving their beasts outside.

For those who cared to pay more, there were two or three rooms in the *fondouk* which you might share with the fleas and rats. I was more anxious to spend the night with the Bedouins in the farthest courtyard, but Chicco interposed, and with significant gestures gave me to understand why it would be better to sleep in a certain room whose door had heavy wooden bolts. I did not, however, retire to my room until late, and spent some time in making friends among these swarthy Africans.

In front of the building was the well where the last comers were engaged in drawing water for themselves and their beasts. I hastened to get a drink, but found the water very nasty, and only bearable when made into coffee. Just inside the entrance was an Eastern store where Arab provisions could be purchased. Sour cakes of doughy brown bread were displayed, dirty-brown salt, olive oil, and, what was more acceptable, fresh eggs. The Moorish proprietor sat aloft cross-legged, and graciously gave the Wanderer about half the value of his money, while Chicco acted as cook. On the other side of the arched passage was a *café*. Here I sat cross-legged among the noisy Moors and sipped my black *Garfoor*. I got involved in an argument about Arabi Pasha and the Mahdi, and thought it advisable to leave and have a turn with the Bedouins.

The farthest courtyard was a picturesque sight now that it was getting dark. Here and there a fire was lit, and round it crouched and lay the Bedouins with their animals. A camel with mouth dripping from the well advanced with stately step and slow, and looked round at the different groups to see where he would be most comfortable. His owner's son, holding on to his tail, drove him up to the family gathering, and down he went on his knees after a little grumbling, and the little brown children were soon climbing all over their *djmil*.

The donkeys at one side and the family camel at the other formed a rampart to protect from thievish neighbours. By means of small bronze coins I soon got the infant section of that family enlisted in my favour, and then squatted down by the camp fire as they cooked their *kous-kousoo*. The conversation was not animated, but it was amusing; the tattoo-marks on the Arabs' arms and faces supplying an interesting topic, and a small brown precocity was delighted when I made imitation tattoo-marks upon his arms with a copying-ink pencil. The Arab damsels sat round the fire cooking the supper.

At last I withdrew, and settled down on my wooden pallet, with my revolver and money-bag under my portmanteau, which served for pillow. I had become somewhat used to ordinary bloodthirsty insect life. The mosquito, the domesticated flea, and its more objectionable partner in crime, might work their wicked wills with impunity—it was a necessary consequence of Oriental life. But at last a horror is found which I cannot away with, a creature which burrows in the flesh and lays its eggs, only to be removed by strong chemicals. This night was made memorable to me by being thus bitten, and for days I was not in a happy frame of mind.

A fierce row at the door in the early morning brought me with a bound to the great wooden bolts, and, opening one of the doors which hung on a single hinge, I found Chicco in a state of excitement. He had some wonderful news for me; I could scarcely believe him. I understood that there was actually an Englishman somewhere, who had just arrived; so I sent Chicco off with a card, and soon followed him. I felt quite elated; so much had happened since I had seen a fellow-countryman, and to meet an Englishman in the Sahel was no ordinary event.

In a small crowd of Arabs outside I saw a white sun helmet, and Chicco violently gesticulating as he handed my card to a personage who came forward to meet me. He lifted his helmet in the correct manner—*vide* well-known pictures—and exclaimed, "Mr. ——, I presume" (or words to that effect). I returned his salute and we shook hands. The initials of this African traveller, however, were not H. M. S.; he was M. Paolo Bonavia, a British subject from Malta, on his way from Tunis to Susa. It was very pleasant to meet even an English-speaking Maltese, and until my *carosse* was ready, I spent a most entertaining ten minutes in hearing news from the outside world in broken English.

My four steeds were not so bright this morning, and on starting showed no anxiety to cover the forty-five miles which lay between us and Tunis.

Before us, to the north, rose the mountains on the Dakkul peninsula, on our left, to the west, the picturesque Zaghowán mountains and Djebel Resass, and far away to the right the snow-white cluster of houses on the blue bay of Hammamet.

We passed our Arab friends of yesternight, the domestic *djmil* swinging along and looking down upon us contemptuously, the one-year-old baby sleeping calmly on the top of the pannier-baskets, its merry sisters running alongside and saluting the *Roumi* mischievously, while papa was in charge of the donkeys in front.

After dragging for miles over heavy red sand, now descending at full speed into a *wady* and crawling up the far bank, now passing among juniper bushes in abundance, we entered a more fertile country, and found ourselves amidst the barley harvest.

Very picturesque scenes surrounded us. Here the dark-skinned gleaners were gathering up the stray ears. An Arab woman with metal ornaments round her face, and loose blue dress, was merrily laughing with her comrade, and the swarthy husband helped a little as each one gathered the sheaves into her bosom.

> "All among the barley,
> Who would not be blithe?"

Even the donkeys could not suppress a merry twinkle in their eyes as they roamed at will over the unenclosed field, while the reapers obeyed the behests of some bright-robed Boaz sitting beneath a neighbouring olive, and, binding up the sheaves, placed them on the donkeys' backs and led them away to the garner.

After a couple of hours we come upon a clump of

dwarf palms, five or six, shivering in the breeze which had sprung up. Here (El Khwin) are the ruins of a village, depopulated, it is said, by a spring sending forth bituminous water. It has since mended its ways. Passing among blazing oleander-bushes of outrageously huge dimensions, we skirted the gardens of Turki, and drove down the long olive grove, whose trees, planted with faultless regularity, stretched far away on either side. Some four miles farther we entered the village of Kroumbália, three and a half hours from Bir-el-Buwita, and here we rested a little. We were opposite the butcher's establishment, which also was the chief and only *café*, and after watering the horses Chicco foraged for Arab bread, eggs, and *mishmash*, and soon I was swallowing hot black coffee of a semi-solid description.

Our surroundings were interesting. Side by side were a few Moorish houses of a tumble-down description, with sunshades or verandahs of rough earth and grass stretching out in front of the doorways, and under these sat and reclined the male inhabitants, leaving their more useful halves, or four-fifths, to work for them.

The owner of the *café* had just killed and skinned a black goat, and was engaged in washing this object. The operation caused painfully intense interest on the part of a white-haired sheep dog, a hungry grey cat who would have liked to come nearer, the row of Moors sitting cross-legged in front of the *café*, and a legion of black flies who covered everything. Yellow and brown cattle, small but sleek, strolled up to the well across the road, and had a good drink at the trough, and then, looking round dreamily with superabundant water streaming from their mouths, they turned their tails upon the infidel consuming *hubz*, and wandered back to their pasture.

Once more we were toiling onwards, and two hours later rolled down to the beach of the Gulf of Carthage. Over the deep blue sea shone out in the far distance across the gulf the bright houses of Goletta, while dimly on the horizon we could just see the familiar isle of Zembra. Here the Zaghowân mountains end, jutting almost into the water at Hammam-el-Enf, the "Bath of the Nose," and along the mountain side we could see the remains of Hadrian's great aqueduct, which conveyed in olden days the waters of Zaghowân to Carthage, and now renovated leads them to Tunis.

According to Davis we should place Curubis here at Hammam-el-Enf, and if this is so, it is the spot to which St. Cyprian was banished for the year preceding his martyrdom. These rugged mountains, this blue bay, must have been very familiar to Thascius Cyprianus. Through a perfect simoon of white dust we drove the last fifteen miles to Tunis. No storm in the desert could surpass the blinding hurricanes of fine sand which hid everything from sight.

At last I get an awful shock. As we approach the "Burnouse of the Prophet," we hear a rumble followed by a roar, a rush of steam, and an engine whistle, and actually a train dashes past us on its way to Rhades! Oh, Shade of Muhammed! to what are we come? Yesterday morn we left the Sanctuary of the Moors, and here is the Flying Caravan of the *Câfr*, within a short hundred miles!

It was in a steam tram-car, a few months later, that I heard this story of an English driver who was sent out from Tyneside when the locomotives were first introduced to this African continent. One day the passengers reported at the terminus that they had run over a camel on the journey. The chief official sent for William Smith, the driver, to give an account of himself. "Yes," he said, "we ran over "the camel, that's certain, but we did it 'clivvor.' Ye "see, the beast was ganning along the line, and a "native had a helter tiv him. When he seed the train "a-coming he harled, and he harled, but the auld "camel wouldna budge from the road. Of course I "whistled tiv him, but it were no use, and as we had "a good head of steam on, why, we went right at him. "The native he screeched, and he ran away across "the country; and when I looked back, well, it were "a funny sight. For all the world, we had just made "the auld camel into a brown dumpling, and I doubt "that native hasn't stopped running yet, nor hollering "nayther."

R

Now we leave the fascinating uncertainty of our life among the Bedouins behind us and we pass with a bound into French civilization, into the wickedest city on earth since the Cities of the Plain were burnt, into Tunisian Paris with its broad streets and huge hotels.

What struck me above everything, however, on arriving at the Grand Hôtel, was the glass bottle of perfectly crystal water in my bedroom. The number of tumblerfuls that I drank that broiling afternoon would endanger my reputation as an advocate of temperance, but allowances must be made for a hundred-mile journey under the African sun in June, and the delicious liquid conveyed from the Zaghowân mountains by Hadrian's Aqueduct.

CHAPTER XXIII.

TUNIS, CARTHAGE, AND BIZERTA.

Morals at Tunis—Scene from hotel windows—The bazaars—Story-tellers—Jew children at school—Serpent-charmers—Author of "Home, sweet Home"—To Carthage by rail—The lost slippers—On the Byrsa—Gulf of Carthage—Æneas—The Tyrians—Hasdrubal—Perpetua and Felicitas—St. Cyprian—St. Augustine—Bizerta—Jacassey.

THE *Burnouse of the Prophet!* Such is the picturesque name which the Moors give to their capital, as it lies dazzling white, stretching out along the shores of El Bahira. The Prophet's cloak, however, covers a city which can scarcely be rivalled in its wickedness. One breathed more freely when, and only when, one had left Tunis behind altogether.

It is not desirable to dwell upon this objectionable subject, the *morale* of Tunis. Those who know the city will know enough of its morals, and those who know neither the city nor its inhabitants are happier in their ignorance.

Odd things have happened here in past days. We are told by the author of the "*État des Royaumes de Barbarie*" (quoted by Mr. Alexander Broadley), how Tatar Dey " enjoyed the rare distinction of being eaten" by his displeased subjects. This was at the close of the seventeenth century. One wonders at their taste in eating a raw Tatar!

Mr. Wood tells us of an event which happened more recently, when he was Consul-general at Tunis. An unfortunate Israelite, by name Samuel Sfez, being badly treated by some Moslems, cursed their faith and abused the Bey. Being dragged before the cadi, he was condemned to die by swallowing molten lead, which should be poured down his throat. On the 17th June, 1857, this was done. His head was severed from his body, and kicked through the city by the boys, and then smashed by the men with stones.* With such zeal for their religion, one would have expected the Tunisians to have reverenced Muhammed's *moral* precepts more than they do.

Another incident. A year or two ago a Jewish boy was playing with some Arab lads outside the Mosque of the Olive Tree. One of the small Moslems, seizing the Jew boy's cap, ran in at one entrance of the mosque and out at the opposite door. The little Jew promptly followed, and was put to death as he came out at the other door.† I am not familiar with the interior of the Olive Tree Mosque.

Among other interesting events during my sojourn

* "Tunis, Past and Present."
† See "Country of the Moors."

here was the shooting down of a man scarcely one hundred yards from us while we were sitting one evening, in front of the hotel.

At Tunis, certainly, there is a gathering of the dregs of degraded humanity, both male and female. St. Paul describes some of the inhabitants very graphically towards the end of the first chapter of his Epistle to the Romans.

But to turn to less unpleasant topics. There is much that is interesting in the capital of Tunisia. Any one landing from a European steamer at Goletta, and coming up to the city for the first time, could not fail to be pleased with his Oriental surroundings, strangely blended with European comfort in his hotel, and many of the advantages of civilization. Leaning out of the windows of the Grand Hôtel one always saw something picturesque. A fine regiment of Zouaves marched past, with their band leading them on with martial strains. Very different are these bronzed soldiers to the shabby little fellows one saw at Sfax, Susa, and Kairwân. A contrast, too, to the feeble soldiers of the Bey, who are simply a laughing-stock, as they limp along in their absurd uniform, or *knit stockings* in their sentry boxes—this really being their usual occupation.

Within the walls the bazaars are very interesting and extensive. I roamed up and down, and sometimes sat in an Arab *café* and watched the Oriental story-teller as, with graphic action and confidential tone, he kept his audience spell-bound. Attendants noiselessly handed coffee round and refilled the pipes, while the entertainment would perhaps be varied by a performance on the *gimbrik* and *bindir*.

Looking in at a door in the Jewish quarter, I found a boys' school, very similar to the Moorish schools at Tripoli. At the feet of their master squatted some twenty little Jews, all roaring the alphabet together: "*Aleph, Beth, Gimel, Daleth, Hé, Wau, Zayin, Heth.*" Then they took a rest, and the master, stick in hand, went on—"*Teth, Yod, Kaph, Lamed, Mem, Nun, Samech, Ayin*," and the infantine chorus broke in again, swaying backwards and forwards. This went on until they got down to "*Resh, Shin, Tau*," and then they began again.

Some snake-charmers were performing in one street, and I was amused at the immense amount of preliminary action indulged in to attract an audience. Spreading a carpet, two disreputable looking Moors sat thereon, one torturing a species of native bag-pipes, the other discoursing those soothing strains which generally proceed from a tambourine. Placing a curious hive-shaped basket on the ground, the chief performer howled and rushed round and round, until he brought the neighbourhood together and disposed them in a circle. Then he addressed a good-sized snake in the basket, and exhorted him, in the Name of the Prophet, to come out and show himself to the Faithful. He emerged slowly, and two smaller ones also wriggled out on to the carpet and produced an uneasy feeling in the front row of bystanders, upon whom they looked round with open mouth and forked tongue, and some of these in consequence strategically moved into a less prominent position.

Seizing the big snake, the charmer held him up by the tail high above his face, and, opening his mouth, pretended he was going to drop him down his throat. Suddenly the snake darted at his eye; he dropped the reptile as if red hot, and rolled over and over on the ground in exquisitely simulated agonies. Money showered into the circle, tambourine and bagpipes kept up their merry discordance, and the crowd grew larger and more interested.

I bore letters of introduction to Herr Nachtigal, the famous African explorer, who lives at Tunis, and I bear a very happy recollection of our brief acquaintance. Herr Nachtigal is one of the greatest living travellers, and has had the highest honours bestowed upon him that Europe could offer. His name has been more recently before the public as having been sent by the German Government to the West Coast. Bismarck has made a wise choice. Since I saw him he has travelled to the Sivan oasis, and interviewed the Senoussian Mahdi at Djardub.

In the English cemetery at Tunis for thirty years have reposed the remains of John Howard Payne, the author of words known wherever the English language is spoken, words which have often caused tears to flow in far distant lands. The author of "Home, sweet Home," died far from home at last. He died here in Tunis, on April 1st, 1852. Colonel Payne was twice American consul here, and his countrymen erected a monument to him in our cemetery. It was but a few days before I arrived from Kairwân, that an American man-of-war had arrived to take John Howard Payne home; home to his own land, to be buried among his own people. The tombstone, which until this year was visited by all English and American travellers, bore these words:—

IN MEMORY OF
COLONEL JOHN HOWARD PAYNE,
Twice Consul of the United States of America for the Kingdom of Tunis,
This stone is here placed by a grateful country.
He died at the American Consulate in this city after a tedious illness, April 1st, 1852.
He was born at the city of Boston, State of Massachusetts, June 8th, 1792.
His fame as a Poet and Dramatist
Is well known wherever the English language is spoken through his celebrated ballad "Sweet Home" and his popular tragedy of "Brutus" and other similar productions.

Around the stone were these lines:

Sure when thy gentle spirit fled
To realms beyond the azure dome,
With arms outstretched God's angels said,
Welcome to Heaven's Home, Sweet Home.

ORIENTAL CONCERT.

Tunis has been so often described, that a detailed account of my four days' stay would scarcely be interesting. A few words, however, as to Carthage. The site of the ancient capital of Africa lies some seven or eight miles north-east of Tunis, overlooking Goletta, or La Goulette, the Tunis port. This is called in Arabic *Halk el Oued*, the *gullet* or throat of that river, which connects the Little Sea (El Bahira), upon which Tunis is built, with the Great Sea.

From Tunis to a stopping place near Carthage one travels now by train! In an open carriage of great width, with verandah above and a continuous balcony along each side, we rode with a score or so of tastefully dressed Moors. The line skirts that huge lake of brackish water which lies between Tunis and the sea and which is known as the Bahira.

In the radiant sunlight the lovely crimson-breasted flamingoes stood fishing in the shallows or flew away in long lines—snowy white one moment, and then, as they wheeled round, changing into a sunset crimson. Quaint old-world birds, with their slim long necks and hooked bills, so Egyptian and strange.

Yonder is the old castle of Shikli, standing solitary on its islet, the Chillon of this lake of Tunis. Soon we swept away from the Bahira and steamed along the plains, where the slow-pacing, forward-stretching camels were moving along; and Bedouin children shouted for joy as the little engine (from

Messrs. Sharp, Stewart, & Co.'s works at Manchester) whirled us first to Malka and then towards Carthage. We passed the lovely house of our consul, Mr. Reade, its gardens shaded by stately cypress and palm, and ablaze with scarlet *gerania*.

The Moors in the train enjoyed the whole thing delightfully; some of them just like children. They would not sit properly like we do, but, putting their slippers on the floor, squatted cross-legged on the seat like rows of tailors. I was immensely tickled by one old Moor, who was so taken up with his ride in the "fire-carriage" that he did not notice that the vibration of the train, slowly but surely, was working his slippers aft along the carriage floor.

"Great Muhammed!" he cried, in a sudden paroxysm of grief. "In the name of the Prophet, where are my *blaghi*?" He thought that the Dog of an Infidel had been playing a joke upon him, until we quietly pointed to him the slippers slowly working their way down the carriage. "Allah be praised!" he remarked quietly.

I was the only passenger to alight at the stopping place near to Carthage, and I salaamed to my Moorish friends as the train trundled along towards Goletta, leaving me alone; there being no station-master or official, and not a soul within sight.

Under the blazing sun I found my way over the mounds which mark the site of great Carthage, in some measure resembling those "Graves of the Gods" at Upsala-Gamla, where Odin and Thor and Freya lie buried. After a fiercely hot climb I stood upon the Byrsa, and rested near the modern buildings of the community of Notre Dame d'Afrique. What a glorious view! and what tremendous associations, as one gazed on scenes which have witnessed the world's history!

From the heights of the Byrsa I looked down upon the Cothon and the Portus Mercatorius, the only distinct signs of Punic Carthage. To the north, in the distance, are the huge underground cisterns, colossal water caverns for the supply of the ancient city. Ruins such as one expected there were none, but everywhere the soil is mixed with pieces of marble and masonry. "*Delenda est Carthago,*" old Cato used to mutter on all occasions. If his shade ever hovers in the neighbourhood it must feel highly gratified, for one could scarcely imagine any city more completely wiped off the face of the earth than Phœnician, Punic, Roman, Byzantine, and Vandal Carthage has been.

And yet the more distant view from the Byrsa must be the same as that which Hannibal, or Augustine, or Okhbah beheld. The great bay of delicious dark blue water, melting into emerald in its shallower parts, stretches to the Great Sea in the north, bounded as of old on its farther side by the dark rugged mountain chain—masses of chocolate-coloured rock piled one behind the other towards

Zaghowân. Over the face of the blue water dark shadows are chased by the breeze as the light cloudlets hurry across the sky.

Yonder, in the roadstead of Goletta, steamers and sailing vessels lie at anchor, and in this clear atmosphere look like toy ships which one could lift out of the water by their masts and put back again. They seem but a stone's throw from the port of Goletta, though they are a mile or so really from its cluster of white houses, and four or five miles from the Byrsa. Where the promontory of El Dakkul ("the strip") joins the mainland I can see the camel track from Kairwân passing out on to the shore and winding beneath the rugged mountains, and a few white dots show the position of the village of Hammam el Enf, where the white dust still whirls in colossal clouds.

This glorious bay, with many another, is compared with the Bay of Naples, but I think the Gulf of Carthage can never be surpassed, as it bathes in African sunlight, dotted here and there with white felucca sails, and stretching to distant Cape Bon and to rocky Zembra down on the horizon.

Would the ships of Æneas, when forsaking poor Dido on her funeral pyre, appear very much unlike that fleet of *balancelles* passing away into the Mediterranean?

Did not those mountains of Zaghowân and Djebel Resass yonder look exactly the same, when the first Phœnician traders found their way hither from Tyre to build them a city to dwell in? It was in the days of Jehu, the son of Jehoshaphat, sovereign over the Nation of Monotheists, that these Baal-worshippers of Tyre brought hither the idols of that deity whose images and altars Jehu was then so zealously breaking down.* The world has grown old since those days. Carthage has often risen and fallen since then.

Arab children play among the ruins, and offer pieces of stone not very different from hundreds of scraps of ruins lying around, and expect to receive a small fortune from the European visitor. One finds it hard to realize that one is walking on the site of busy streets, and within the huge walls of great Carthage. The gardens of the monastery of St. Louis are filled with Roman and Phœnician inscriptions, and in their museum lamps, mosaics, and stone balls used in the *catapultæ;* and as one sauntered under the cypress trees and palms, one knew that here was the site of the Temple of Æsculapius, where Hasdrubal's wife slew her sons and then threw herself into the flames rather than fall into the hands of the conquerors.

Fat-tailed sheep, and bullocks no bigger than small donkeys, roam among the ruins, obtaining a scanty meal, under the charge of Arab shepherds enveloped in their rough *baracans.* The black goat-

* See Bosworth Smith's "Carthage and the Carthaginians."

hair tents on the side of the Byrsa are the homes of those Arab women yonder who are gathering in a thin crop of golden barley on the Magaria while their little ones roll about in front of the tents. The corn is pulled up by the roots and carried off on donkey-back.

It is hard to realize that this is the city of Hamilcar Barca, of Hannibal, and of Hasdrubal, and that this was the scene of the fierce siege by the younger Scipio, who left not one stone upon another in this Capital of Africa. Julius Cæsar intended to rebuild Carthage, but the execution of the project was left to his nephew Augustus.

It was in yonder elliptical excavation near the railway line that the great amphitheatre stood, and there Perpetua and Felicitas witnessed their good confession when they were cast to the maddened beast which was to gore them to death, and finally were slain by the gladiator's sword. This was upon Geta's birthday, A.D. 202.

Not far from this spot the great Cyprian was beheaded fifty years later. New Carthage was indeed the stronghold of African Christianity, and it was in this city that the great Council was held in 397, A.D., when under Augustine, the Canon of Scripture was in great measure decided, and the Bible was given to the World by the Church. The sirocco-blast of Islam has long since strewn the ruins of Christianity on the African sands, and now there is no such thing as a

Moorish Church in Africa, where once Christianity flourished.*

It was a few days after my wanderings amid the Carthaginian ruins that I sailed away down the Gulf of Tunis. Gazing for the last time upon old Kart-Hadact, upon the Byrsa and the white houses of Sidi bou Said, I felt I had been privileged to stand upon ground almost holy with the associations of the world's history. The year before, looking up at Mount Ida, and upon the plains of Troy stretched out before me, I had felt as I feel now, that if I had visited such scenes a few years ago I might have been a more enthusiastic classic, and certainly a more interested student of ancient history.

About forty miles along the coast towards Algeria is the town and great inland lake of Bizerta. The importance of this vast land-locked harbour, containing some *fifty square miles of anchorage*, has been terribly overlooked by our Government. The French army now occupies Tunis, which is described in this year's "Whitaker" as "an informally annexed dependency of France." The Bizerta lake, at a comparatively small cost, can be converted into a great naval depôt, from which men-of-war may steam out any moment and completely block this narrow part of the Mediterranean, nullify our advantages in

* See "History of North African Church," by Julius Lloyd (S.P.C.K.).

holding Malta, and practically close up for us the Suez Canal. Some day, when it is too late, England will awake to find Bizerta another Toulon, and Malta and the highway to India at the mercy of our Gallic friends, the proprietors of that French lake commonly known as the Mediterranean.

We came on deck after dinner, as we were approaching Bizerta, and soon I was in a boat manned by Sicilian boatmen, pulling for the shore.

Upon this last stage of my journey I was no longer alone, but there was with me one whose name has already been mentioned several times, and whose handiwork in this volume conveys a better idea of many scenes than any words of mine. My artist-friend, A. F. Jacassey, whom I had met in Tunis, was with me now, and he had some Sicilian jokes with our boatmen. We glided over a calm sea, and in the depths beneath us could see the rocks and seaweed, and the fish looking up at us in piscine wonder. We almost seemed to be floating in the air. We sailed under the *kasbah*, and gliding into the harbour, we landed in the Moorish Venice with its waterways and bridges.

We strolled through the quaint narrow streets, and under the flying buttresses reaching from house to house, reminding one of Tripoli. We crossed the main channel which leads into Lake Tinga—the proper name for the great land-locked harbour with its fifty square miles of anchorage. We passed over the connecting arm of the sea by an ancient bridge, and then out through the city gate, where Moors were congregated, and sitting cross-legged discussed their neighbours' affairs. Returning through the town we crossed over another arm of the sea by a narrow bridge some seventy yards in length, about five feet above the water, made merely of planks resting on trestles, with no railing to prevent one falling overboard. We are in a country of teetotallers.

Sitting at a Moorish *café* we sipped our little cups of Arab coffee, and admired the bright dresses of the crowd around us, lit up now by lamps hung upon the walls. It was our last night in a real Moorish town, and it was certainly a romantic scene, the last I should see for some time in Tunisia. Gliding out to the *Ville d'Oran* over the dark smooth sea, Jacassey and I each took an oar, and chatted with our Sicilian boatmen about a recent wreck on Cani Island. At the entrance to the harbour, a red lighthouse on its port side and a green light to starboard were reflected in the calm sea, and with the crescent moon they formed three streaks of light on the gently heaving surface—red, green, and white.

Half a mile out to sea lay our vessel, with its long row of bright cabin lights all reflected in the still dark water below; and as we approached her, great phantom barges glided slowly past us towards the

S

harbour. Their cargoes had been stowed on board the *Ville d'Oran*, and stretching out their huge sails to catch the slightest breath of air, they crept silently homewards. " Farewell. Tunisia. Good-bye to the Land of the Bey."

CHAPTER XXIV.

THE HOME OF AUGUSTINE.

Algeria—Al Kalah—Bonah—Ubba—Broken cisterns—Statue of St. Augustine—His "Confessions"—Thagaste—Monica—Carthage—Milan—The great Bishop of Hippo Regius—His life and death—A swim—Fishing boats—A rude picture—Our drive—Farewell to Africa—Sardinia—Straits of Bonifacio—Corsica—Ajaccio—Napoleon—Beaune—Snores—Rhone—Musical mastication—Across *La Manche*—Westminster Abbey.

EACH time I have sailed along this Algerian coast and in the distance seen the "City of Jujube Trees" nestling under the shadow of the African hills, I have longed to be on shore, to wander among scenes which seemed familiar even though unvisited—the spot where the great Augustine wrote his "Confessions," and spent thirty-seven years of that most valuable life.

At last the wish was to be gratified. The early morning light dimmed the brightest star, and, tinging the eastern sky with orange, gradually lit up the dark mountains, till at last the fiery sun came rushing up from the glistening waves. I turned over in my hammock slung on the upper deck of the

Ville d'Oran, to see now no longer the Tunisian coast, but Algeria on our port beam.

About 4 a.m. our engines slowed and stopped, and we lay off the town of La Calle—the Moorish Al Kalah. Wooded slopes rose far above the white French town, and here and there on the mountain side were perched yellow villas. Not a minaret, not a Moorish building to be seen; in fact, nothing to show one that it was Africa. We lay-to long enough to impress the scene upon our minds—the long blue waves swelling lazily towards the stony beach, the white houses clustered together under the shadow of the hills—and then we steamed away past the coral fleet here at work, until, four or five hours later, we were approaching the town of Bonah or Bone, lying in its great bay, its background of mountains rising from the blue Mediterranean.

Beneath the *kasbah* or fort which dominates the town and harbour, two long white piers stretch out into the sea—an unusual sight on the North African coast. This is the first port where we have been able to enter and make fast alongside a quay.

A crowd of Frenchmen, Maltese, and Italians collected as the *Ville d'Oran* glided into the harbour, and as we came alongside, a turbaned policeman cleared a passage to the gangway. Practically we were in France now—*boulevards*, hôtels, *rues*, churches, *cafés*, shops—and scarcely a vestige of the *Mauresque* to be seen anywhere.

Bonah is certainly a charming modern town, but it is difficult to believe that one is not on the Riviera in the *Grande Place* at Toulon, with the mountains behind and the blue sea before.

The ruins of the Roman town of Hippo Regius (the Carthaginian Ubba) lie a couple of miles to the southeast of Bone. Hither we drove in the blazing sun, but shaded by the huge white umbrella of our smart *calèche*. The white hard road passes between lofty hedges of prickly pear, aloes, and acanthus, and is often shaded by veteran olive trees with gnarled branches and dark leaves. Our *cocher* drew rein at the foot of the hill upon which Ubba once stood, and said that his steeds would not venture further upon that broiling day. Jacassey and I, however, were not deterred, and, following the winding road upwards, we arrived at last at the bronze statue of Augustine, and climbing further to the very summit of the Ubban Hill, we stood and gazed at one of those glorious panoramic views which owe so much to a clear atmosphere and the rich colouring of a southern clime.

The sun was at its meridian, and it poured in its scorching strength upon us and upon the distant red roofs of Bonah below us in the great bay, which stretches round in a long sweep, its two piers running out far into the dark blue sea. Behind us a long valley opened towards the interior, a white road passing along it towards Souk Ahras. Massive hills rose on either side of the level ground in this valley, where cultivation is carried on as if in France.

As we sat on some stones—the remnants of Hippo Regius—the ants ran wildly hither and thither, and a hum of insect life pervaded the air. A chameleon, who was startled by the intrusion of the two wanderers, dodged up a tree and peeped down at us blushingly.

The whole soil here is formed of stones and concrete, marble and white plaster, but the only substantial relics to be seen of Hippo Regius were its huge cisterns on the hillside, the great reservoirs some seventy or eighty feet deep. At one time these were massively arched over, like the Carthaginian cisterns, in order to exclude this African sun, but here and there the roof has fallen in.

Their depths are now inhabited by some Bedouins, and no longer contain the dark cool water. As we looked over we saw below us the whole family of an Algerian Arab, with his children and female relatives. The usual yell of "*Roumi! Roumi!*" to which one is now accustomed, came up from the cavernous depths, as the brightly attired damsels pretended to hide their faces and peeped through their fingers. We found our way into the cisterns from the hillside, and here obtained an idea of their stupendous massiveness.

The scene was very picturesque as we looked upwards. Great masses of prickly pear hung down in heavy festoons from above, and foliage and verdure spread itself everywhere among the ruins. The Bedouin children watching us timidly and not heeding the warning scolding voice of their dark-eyed mothers, added colour and life to the already romantic scene. Just above the cisterns has been raised in modern times a bronze statue of *El Roumi 'l Kebir* * (as the Moors call Augustine), encircled by iron railings. It is not handsome, being less than life size, and neither worthy of the place nor of him whom it is supposed to represent.

And this is almost the scene he beheld when he wrote his "City of God" and his "Confessions," though then around him would rise the houses and churches of the first city in Africa, for M. de la Primaudaie assures us that in Augustine's days Carthage was often considered second to Hippo Regius in prosperity and influence.

Away over those hills is Thagaste, now Souk Ahras, where Augustine spent those early days so familiar to us through his "Confessions," as he studied the hateful Greek and was guilty of the boyish theft he afterwards laments.

There Monica, the pattern of loving mothers, watched over and prayed for that boy who was to have such an influence upon the world.

At Carthage we looked upon the scenes of his youth, where Manichæism and sin bid fair to mar that useful life, and where Monica was assured by

* "The very great Stranger."

a certain Bishop that the child of so many tears could not perish.

At Milan, again, it is not so very long since we beheld scenes which were very familiar to Augustine, when under Ambrose he found Peace in the Truth, or walking in that garden on the Campagna he saw the distant snow-capped Alps beyond Maggiore, Lugano, and Como, when he was aroused by the "Take up and read, take up and read;" and here we think of him returning to his Africa from yonder distant horizon, motherless now, but no longer Godless.

Monica, that devoted mother, had lived to see her son a Christian, but she had been laid to rest at Ostia. She was not permitted to see her Augustine Bishop of Hippo Regius, and the leading mind of the African Church. Often would Augustine's eyes fill with tears when writing his "Confessions," within a few yards of the spot where we stood, for he would look out over the same deep blue sea shimmering under that blazing sun, and his thoughts would fly to the northern continent where he had left his mother Monica sleeping near the yellow Tiber. Here in the streets that then covered this wooded hillside he might be seen in the black dress of the Eastern cœnobites, and here, living a life of mild asceticism, Augustine for thirty-five years ruled the Church in Africa.

On August the 28th, 430, Augustine here breathed

FELLOW PASSENGERS ON THE VILLE D'ORAN
MAL DE MER.

his last, as Genseric's Vandals were battering in the gates of Hippo Regius. A double blow was given to the Church in Africa when these Arian Vandals sacked and utterly destroyed the noble city, bereft now of its spiritual head.

Such thoughts swept through our mind as we sat amid the ruins of Hippo; and at last we descended, leaving behind us the monument of the great Evangelical Catholic of the early Church, as it stands above the huge reservoirs of those old days. Now we read with redoubled interest that masterpiece of autobiography, a history which proves the truth there asserted:

"*Inquietum est cor nostrum donec requiescat in Te*" (*Conf.* i. 1).

The "Confessions of Augustine" are dear to me, even as they were dear to my fellow-traveller.

Jacassey and I had a good swim together that afternoon at the end of one of the long piers. In spite of African sharks we plunged down into the crystal depths of the dark blue water, and swam out to a buoy, but dressed hurriedly on coming out of the water to avoid the blisters that the terrific sun threatened to inflict upon European skins. We had rowed out from the inner harbour, and now, landing at the lighthouse, we watched the *balancelles*, the *lanca di pesce*, and, the *coralliere* sweeping homewards before the breeze.

Lovely, graceful boats they were, each borne swiftly

onwards by the huge Venetian sail swelling out before the fresh breeze. The whole fleet were making for the harbour, and one by one they came along, racing over the rollers, closely shaving the pier-head, and then hauling down the great sail as they glided on towards the inner harbour. We could almost shake hands with the crews of picturesque Sicilians and Maltese as the boats rushed past us. Down in the bottom of the *lanca di pesce* leapt the silvery fish just caught, and in the *coralliere* heavy masses of coral lay piled as ballast and cargo.

The owner of B 86 wishes to immortalize himself. As his *balancelle* came on plunging and tossing over the white-crested waves, we saw an heroic figure depicted in colours on the great sail swelling out before the wind. Like an argosy of old with striking scenes depicted on silken mainsail, the fishing-boat came racing up in the breeze, twenty more close behind. Horror of horrors, what do we see? Oh degraded Sicilian, or barbarous Maltese, we are ashamed of thee. The huge sail of B 86 bears the picture of a man with his fingers and thumbs joined but extended in front of his nasal organ!

We had an enjoyable ride through the suburbs of Bonah, with their exquisite gardens. Towards the mountains we drove, past Moorish burial-grounds and under dark cypresses; then, winding upwards as we turned seawards, we found ourselves near the *kasbah*, looking down upon the rocks far below, where the transparent blue waves were curling over, and a mule was being washed by a negro. The negro tucked up his petticoats between his legs and splashed salt water over the mule's face to improve its complexion. The mule found it monotonous, and was backing away when we last saw it. Then, it seems, we fell asleep, and our drive subsequently was not a good investment. This is the consequence of getting up at 3.30 a.m.

As the dark hills of Africa sank into the sea that evening I felt sad. Since we sailed under the mountains near Tangiers on my journey out how much had happened! Jacassey tried to cheer me with Arabic stories, but not until two argumentative Frenchmen in their intense excitement nearly got to blows at the dinner table did I forget my sorrow. I was almost hoping that the upholder of the merits of Algeria as opposed to France would have tweaked his compatriot's nose, or jumped down his throat.

We coasted Sardinia next day. Along the face of its precipitous cliffs, as they tower more than a thousand feet from the sea, floated long lines of feathery clouds, just as they cling to those heights of the Bürgenstock, rising precipitously from the *Vier-wald-stätter see*, almost a counterpart of these Sardinian cliffs.

As we ran for Ajaccio that evening we had an exquisite sunset. The mountains of Corsica pierced the clouds behind the town which is the birthplace of the great Napoleon, and upon the summits of the highest the snow rested in large fields, and burned a lovely rose colour as the sun sank into an unruffled green sea; and soon Isola Sanguinaire and the rugged mountains encircling the great bay stood out in black shadows against the sky, downy streaks of cloud strata lying along their sides weird and ghostly in the half light. While we wandered in the streets of Ajaccio a man was assassinated within a few yards of us.

Jacassey and I wished to spend a day at Beaune, that we might visit the celebrated Hôtel Dieu. We travelled from Marseilles through the night in company with a dark-skinned Moor bound for Vichy. The splendour of his snores astonished us. He snored in pure Arabic, and almost caused the carriage to vibrate with his musical efforts. At times one expected that the roof of his mouth would finally have given way and disappeared down his throat, and yet he began again with renewed vigour, as if determined to drown the rattle of the train.

In the early morning we were rolling onwards by the banks of the swollen Rhone, whose brown waters here are strangely different in colour and volume to the stream issuing from its colossal icy birthplace at the foot of the Füreka Pass.

We wandered in the quaint streets of Beaune, and were charmed with its cathedral, and especially the ancient hospital for the aged and sick. They live in the fifteenth century in that quiet and picturesque old town. What an unwelcome change next day to the glare and roar of gay Paris!

In the Champs Elysées was being held an *Exposition Alimentaire*, and as an inducement to enter the flowery placard announced a *Fête pantagruelique*, and even *Dégustation gratuite*. No wonder that the Public paid its franc, and munched vigorously to the "Overture to Faust," which the band of the 28th in their gay uniform was rendering with Parisian brilliance.

My friend Jacassey was on his way to New York. I too had very welcome duties which summoned me northwards to my insular home. Unwillingly I parted with my cosmopolitan companion, in hopes of meeting again on African soil, and the next morning I presented my baggage to English custom-house officers.

Some Parisians who had never crossed *La Manche* before travelled up to town with me on their way to the Fisheries Exhibition.

They were much excited on being in a strange country for the first time. They beheld a number of policemen on the platform of a suburban station. "*Voilà*," cried one, "*les gendarmes anglais!*" They all rushed to the window. "*Parbleu!* How big! *Mais où sont les épées?*"

* * * * *

From the Djâma 'l Kebir of Kairwân to Westminster Abbey, what a change! With strong feelings of gratitude, I found myself in the glorious old fane, musing over the events of the last few weeks. There I again offered my humble and hearty thanks to the kind Providence which had brought me safely through all.

Deep in thought, I almost forgot where I was, and there seemed to ring in my ears the long wailing cry of the Mueddin from the great *Minar* of Okhbah's mosque—

> "*Allahu-ach-Kebar.*
> "*Allahu-ach-Kebar.*
> "*Es sallè kheir min en nûm.*"

> "GOD IS MOST GREAT!
> "GOD IS MOST GREAT!
> "PRAYER IS BETTER THAN REST!"

INDEX.

A

Abdullah ben Said, of Khartoum, 58–63
Abdullah ben Sherîf, 212
Abdul Moulir, house of, at Sfax, 141
Ablutions before prayer, 86
Achmet el Hadji (the renegade) of Kairwân), 196
Achmet Rassim, the Pasha of Tripoli, 107–111
Addar Ras (Cape Bon), 17, 18, 252
Adrumetum, 148
Adzân, the, 44, 167, 172, 270
Africa Cape, 144–5
Ain Zhara (the Saharan spring), 96, 102
Ajaccio, 267
Algeria, 259–267
Am Roos, 79
Asfachus, 133–143
Augustine, 254, 263–265
Azhar, the Mosque, at Cairo, 180

B

Bahira, El, 243, 249
Barth at Bir-el-Buwita, 233
Baruti, the well of, at Kairwân, 208
Baracan, the, 73
Bective, Lord and Lady, at Kairwân, 7
Bedouins, 101–156, 229, 230, 234–236

Beaune, 268
Bindiggah, the, 101
Bir-el-Buwita, 232–242
Bizerta, 255–258
Black Village, the, at Tripoli, 111–115
Bonah or Bone, 260–267
Bon Cape, 17, 18
Borac Al, preface, and 96–106
Bordj Bou Leilah, 89 *note*
Broadley, Mr. Alexander, 8, 179 *note*, etc.
British Association, paper on Kairwân at, 1
Byrsa, the, at Carthage, 252

C

Café at Kairwân, 164
Camels, on, 47–52
Cairo and Kairwân, 180
Calle, La, 260
Carpenter, Mr. H., F.R.I.B.A., on the great mosque of Kairwân, 3, 179–181
Carthage, 249–255
Carthage, Gulf of, 17, 240, 252
Christianity and Muhammedanism, 48–52
Cicalas, 162
Comino and Cominotto, 20–21
Constantinople, Mosque of Santa Sophia at, 41
Cordova and Kairwân, 3, 179–182
Curubis, 240
Cyprian, St., 240, 254

D

Dakkul promontory, the, 18, 149, 237, 252
Djâma 'l Kebir, the, at Kairwân, 3, 168-182, 218-219; (For other "Djâmas" see "Mosque")
Djerbah, Island of, 126
"Dunsford's" at Valetta, 25

E

Esparto market at Tripoli, 47
Esran, the Sheykh El, 212
Etienne, Gen., leads French troops through, 7

F

Fatihat, Al, 219
Fez (Sheshiyah, Chacich, or Tarboosh), 77, 192
Filfla, Island of, 27
Fior' del Mondo, El, 19
Fondouk, a night in a, 233-238
"Frederic" (Mr. F. Warrington, of Tripoli), 64
Funeral, Muhammedan, 137

G

Galita and Galitona, 17
Ghabes, 128-131
Gibraltar and Kairwân, 3, 15
Gimbrih and *bindir*, 77, 164
Goletta, (La Goulette, or Halk el Oued), 249
Gozo, 19, 20
Guerin, Victor, on Kairwân, 9, 177
Gulf of Carthage, 17

H

Hammam at Sfax, 140
Hammam el Enf, 240
Hammamet, Town of Doves, 18, 232, 238
Halk el Oued, 249
Halfa, Souk-el- (Tripoli), 49
Harêm, a Tripolitan, 94
Hannibal, 145, 251, 253
Hasdrubal, 253, 254
Hermitage, the (Tripoli), 65
Hippo Regius, 261-265
Homt-es-Souk, 126

J

Jacassey, Mr. A. F., visits Kairwân in 1881, 8; article in *Harper*, 8 *note;* 190 *note*, etc.

K

Kafayat, well of (Kairwân), 208
Kalah, Al, 260
Kairwân—Generally, 1-9, 159-221
  Bazaars, 183-197
  Bird's-eye view from Minar of Great Mosque, 172, 173
  Gates, Bab-el-Djedid, 204, 214
    Bab-el-Djulludin, 167, 200, 210, 221
    Bab el Kasla, 203
    Bab el Khaukh, 201 *note*, 207
    Bab el Tunes, 203, 210, 221
    Khaukhat, 205
  Mosques—
    Mosque and tomb of the 'Companion,' 211-214
    Mosque of Emir Abada, 216-217
    Mosque of the Olive Tree, 204
    The Great Mosque (Djâma 'l Kebir), 168-182
    Prayer Chamber, 175-182
    Maksoorah, 178
    Alembar, 178
    Minar (inscription on), 171
    Mihrâb, 175, 177-182, 199
    Pillars, 176 and *note*, 179 and *note*
    Pillar-curse, 176
    Pillars of purity, 176

INDEX.

Zaouias of Kairwân—
  Abd-el-Kadr el Ghelani, 202
  Tidjania, 205
  Aïssaouia, 204, 215
  (Inscription upon latter, 204)
Suburbs of Kairwân—
  Jibleyeh, 203, 216
  Kabliyeh, 162, 204
Walls of Kairwân, 199–206
Kerkena, sponge islands of, 133, 142
Khwin, El, 239
Kroumbalia, 239
Kuss-kuss-ôo, 89, etc.

L

Legmi (tears of the date), 80
Lotos-eaters, island of, 125

M

Mahdi, the, of the Soudân, 104 *note*, 197, 206
Mahdi, the Senoussian, 103, 104 *note*
Mahdi, the, of Mahhdia, 145
Mahhdia, 144–146
Maltese islands, the, 19–27
Maltese, the, in Africa, 55
Marriage, an Oriental, 37
Marábout, 34 *note*
Medressa, 2, 24
Menarah, 231
Membar, 42
Mesheyah, the, 30, 72, 98
Mirage, 143, 223
Mihrâb, 41
Minar, 45
Monica, 263
Monastir, 146
Moureddin, 155
Mosque, interior of the, 41–42
Mosques of
  Tripoli—
    Djâma 'l Gordji, 41–46
    Djâma Shaib el Ain, 85
    Djâma Bashaw, 85
    Mosque and Marábout of Dragut the Corsair, 86

Mosques of
  Sfax—
    (Djâma 'l Bou Shouîsba, Djâma 'l Kebîr), 139
  Susa—
    (Djâma 'l Natreddin and Djâma 'l Kebîr), 148
  Tunis—
    (Mosque of the Olive Tree), 204
  Kairwân—
    Djâma 'l Kebîr, 168–182
    Mosque of Abada, 216–217
    Mosque of the Companion, 211–214
    Mosque of Olive Tree, 204
Mugreb, land of the, 39 *note*
Muhammed ben Aissa, 215
Muhammed of Kairwân, 168, etc.

N

Nachtigal, Dr., 103, 247
Nuklah, up a, 104, 105

O

Okhbah, Okbar, or Ogbah, 4, 5, 181
Ortegal, Cape, 13
Ousselat mountains, 2, 159, 174

P

Pantellaria, Island of, 18
Payne, Colonel (author of "Home, Sweet Home"), his grave at Tunis, 247, 248
Perpetua and Felicitas, 254
Promontorium Mercurii, 18

Q

Quadrifrontal Roman arch at Tripoli, 31, 32 and *notes*

T

R

Rabato, 20
Rae, Mr., Edward (author of "Country of the Moors"), 6, 7, 32 *note*, 94, 179, 193, 195, 199, 204, 205 *note*, etc.
Rosetta or Raschid to succeed Kairwân, 5
Ruspina, 146

S

Sabra or Sabrata, 170 and *note*
Sahel, El, 153-162
Sahosa, 96-106, 128, 129 and *note*
Saharan canal, 129 *note*
Sangue Christiania, 88
Sardinia, coasting, 267
Selmûn, palace, 21
Schools at Tripoli, 82-84; at Tunis, 246
Scripture references—
   Gen. xlv. 27 (wagons), 156
   Deut. xi. 10 (watering with foot), 91
   Deut. xxv. 4 (unmuzzled ox), 91
   Ruth ii. 3 (barley harvest), 238
   2 Kings x. 28 (Jehu and Baal), 253
   Matt. vi. 19 (digging through to steal), 79
   Matt. ix. 17 (leather bottles), 138
   Matt. xxiv. 17 (housetop), 80
   Matt. xxv. 5-6 (the Bridegroom cometh), 39
   Luke vii. 12 (funeral), 136
   Luke x. 19 (the Aïssaouia), 213
   John x. 14 (the Good Shepherd), 224
   Acts xxvii. 17 (the Syrtis), 124
   Acts xxvii. 41 (St. Paul's Bay, Malta), 22
Seven Capes, promontory of the (Ras Sebbah Rous), 16
Sfax, Sfakkus, or Asfackus, 133-143
Shaôushs at Sfax, 141
Shikli, castle of, 249

Shotts or Sebkas (freshwater lake), 129, 157
To be made use of for inland sea), 130 *note*
The Sebka Kelibia, 157
The Sebka Sidi el Hani, 157
Shreefs, or sherifs, at Sfax, 139
Spartel, Cape, 14
Sidi el Hani, 158, 159
St. Paul's Bay, and scene of his shipwreck, 21, 22
Snails in the Desert, 162
Souk el Djâma, at Tripoli, 69
Souk Ahras (Thagaste), 261
Susa, or Sousse, 147-152
Svinge, 107
Syrtis, Greater and Lesser, 124

T

Tah Hona, 137
Tarabolos Gharb, 28, 123
Tangiers, 14
Tatar Dey, 244
Temple, Sir G. H., at Kairwân, 6
Tinga, Lake, 256
Tinne, history of Miss, 58-63
Toure, a pariah, 76
Tripoli, 28-123
   Bird's-eye view from Minaret, 45, 46
   Mosques, 41-46; 85, 86
   Walls and gates, 89-94
Tunisia, 127-258
Tunis, 245-248
Turki, 239
Turkish troops at Tripoli, 66, 67

U

Ubba (Hippo Regius) 261-265

V

Valetta, 22-26

W

Waregrans, Dr. Tristram and the, 225–229

Z

Zaghowân mountains, 149, 174, 237, 240, 252
Záouias (head-quarters of Moslem confraternities), at Kairwân, 202–4
Záouia of
   Abd-el-Kadr el Ghelani, 202
   Muhammed ben Aïssa, 204, 215
   The Tidjania, 203
Zembra and Zembrotta, 17, 240, 252
Zemzem and Kafayal, 208
Zhara Ain, 267

FINIS.

www.ingramcontent.com/pod-product-compliance
Lightning Source LLC
Chambersburg PA
CBHW030816230426
43667CB00008B/1244